ROUTLEDGE LIBRARY EDITIONS: CONTINENTAL PHILOSOPHY

Volume 9

QUESTIONING DERRIDA

QUESTIONING DERRIDA
With his replies on philosophy

Edited by
MICHEL MEYER

LONDON AND NEW YORK

First published in 2001 by Ashgate Publishing Ltd

This edition first published in 2018
by Routledge
2 Park Square, Milton Park, Abingdon, Oxon OX14 4RN

and by Routledge
711 Third Avenue, New York, NY 10017

Routledge is an imprint of the Taylor & Francis Group, an informa business

© 2001 Michel Meyer

All rights reserved. No part of this book may be reprinted or reproduced or utilised in any form or by any electronic, mechanical, or other means, now known or hereafter invented, including photocopying and recording, or in any information storage or retrieval system, without permission in writing from the publishers.

Trademark notice: Product or corporate names may be trademarks or registered trademarks, and are used only for identification and explanation without intent to infringe.

British Library Cataloguing in Publication Data
A catalogue record for this book is available from the British Library

ISBN: 978-1-138-06315-0 (Set)
ISBN: 978-1-315-10580-2 (Set) (ebk)
ISBN: 978-1-138-29646-6 (Volume 9) (hbk)
ISBN: 978-1-138-29647-3 (Volume 9) (pbk)
ISBN: 978-1-315-10002-9 (Volume 9) (ebk)

Publisher's Note
The publisher has gone to great lengths to ensure the quality of this reprint but points out that some imperfections in the original copies may be apparent.

Disclaimer
The publisher has made every effort to trace copyright holders and would welcome correspondence from those they have been unable to trace.

Questioning Derrida
With his replies on philosophy

Edited by
MICHEL MEYER

Ashgate
Aldershot • Burlington USA • Singapore • Sydney

© Michel Meyer 2001

All rights reserved. No part of this publication may be reproduced, stored in a retrieval system, or transmitted in any form or by any means, electronic, mechanical, photocopying, recording or otherwise without the prior permission of the publisher.

Published by
Ashgate Publishing Ltd
Gower House
Croft Road
Aldershot
Hants GU11 3HR
England

Ashgate Publishing Company
131 Main Street
Burlington, VT 05401-5600 USA

Ashgate website: http://www.ashgate.com

British Library Cataloguing in Publication Data
Questioning Derrida : with his replies on philosophy
   1.Derrida, Jacques, 1930- 2.Philosophy, French - 20th
   century
   194

Library of Congress Control Number: 00-134472

ISBN 0 7546 1397 6

Printed and bound by Athenaeum Press, Ltd.,
Gateshead, Tyne & Wear.

Contents

Preface		*vii*
1	From Grammatology to Problematology *Michel Meyer*	1
2	The Delay of Consciousness *Daniel Giovannangeli*	6
3	The Decision of Analogy: A Remark on Derrida, Reader of Plato *Karel Thein*	14
4	Daydream *John Sallis*	29
5	Deconstruction, Ontology, and Philosophy of Science: Derrida on Aristotle *Christopher Norris*	39
6	Points and Counterpoints: Between Hegel and Derrida *Arkady Plotnitsky*	66
7	Derrida and Science *Christopher Johnson*	84
8	As if it were Possible, "within such limits" … *Jaques Derrida*	96
Index		*120*

Preface

In this volume, we have asked some of the most prominent philosophers to write about some aspects of Derrida's philosophical perspective. Some have commented a given topic, others have defended an alternative view.

Questioning Derrida implies a certain conception of philosophy as questioning, now called 'problematology'. The exposition of this new way of doing philosophy opens the volume.

Finally, Derrida has replied to all contributors and has thereby made more precise what he means by philosophy.

Michel Meyer

Chapter 1
From Grammatology to Problematology

Michel Meyer

> I try to write (in) the space in which is posed the question of speech and meaning.
> (J. Derrida, *Positions*)

Derrida's work testifies to the problematic state of contemporary thought. It is an appeal to an answer, even if the assertion of such a problematicity is already an answer. It is the positive counterpart to what is usually called "deconstruction". It highlights the necessity of a reconstruction in philosophy, to use Dewey's phrase, as much as it may also adduce a reason to think that such a reconstruction is as vain as it is impossible. On my view at least, Derrida's project contributes to a refoundation of philosophy, because it shows that the traditional views on foundation in philosophy are not only exhausted, but rest on illusory grounds. The rejection of foundationalism in philosophy would have to be equated with the impossibility of any future philosophy at large if there were no other alternative than the traditional conception of reason and language, on which all Western thought has rested since Plato. Deconstruction would be purely nihilistic – and negative – if it could not lead to an alternative way of thinking.

What proposal could be done in favor of an another view, departing radically from the ontologico-propositionalist conception by which Western thought has defined itself?

In order to answer the question of what is first in thought, we should first ask that very question. And what is first, in such a question, if not questioning? Any other answer would, as an answer, presuppose questioning, and could not be first if it did not assert the primacy of questioning. Questioning is then the true and only possible starting point for thought and philosophy. It is a different one from all those proposed by Western thought: God, or the human subject for instance, have been the traditional answers, but they can only serve as foundations if the question of what is foundational is raised and deemed worth asking. Thereby, we fall back on questioning. Let us notice that the rejection of the question of what is first is already an answer to it, even though it would be an answer which, as a matter of fact, would disavow its name. We could add that to question the fact that questioning is primary would simply confirm questioning in its priority and its role.

Would Derrida consider such a question worth asking? Probably not, if it is raised within the framework of traditional thought, in which questioning comes after the "answers", called the propositions. In such a propositionalist framework, the foundationalist problematic leads to the eradication of problematicity as criterion of answerhood, that is of propositionality. But as a real question, posed without prejudice, that is without any presupposed view (answer), the question of what is first is an authentic question, which is important to raise. My answer is probably less Socratic than Derrida's, who keeps questioning alive in a constant movement of "*différance*", while I have chosen[1] to articulate answers and questions and to make this difference the crucial one.

Before tackling the issue of *différance*, I would like to stress the importance of raising the question of a true starting point in philosophy. Such a question may sound a reminiscence of some superseded problematic. The Sophists also thought that way, and Renaissance philosophers did too, as well as all skeptic thinkers in times of radical change and collapse of multisecular world-views. But those skeptic philosophers were superseded in turn. Philosophy cannot do without grounding its answers, and does not accept opinion, *doxa*, and in general, opposed and opposable standpoints. When everything turns out problematic, some new foundation is required to provide answers. The present situation is no less different. Since Marx, Nietzsche, Freud and Darwin, everything in culture and values has revealed itself problematic, even the tradition which is built on the eradication of the problematic as criterion of answerhood, of true propositionality. The solution that consists of putting forth some being or Being itself, God or the human subject, won't do any more. *Différance* can be interpreted as the process by which such an unsuitability or impossibility is revealed. We should recall that Nietzsche, Marx and Freud did not only bring to light some new crisis of or within Western thought, but they attacked the very ideal of Western thought, its innermost nature. All Western thought has been erected on the presupposed ideal of necessity or apodicticity, of unicity against multiplicity. Socratic questioning must give way to Platonic answering. The Theory of Ideas represents the first embodiment of propositionalism. To Socratic or sophistic questioning, which allows for alternatives, Plato replied by saying that we cannot have A and not-A, that necessarily one of them must prevail. Alternatives came then to be excluded, and the principle of their exclusion was codified by Aristotle as the supreme principle of *logos* (*Metaphysics*, book *gamma*). The necessity of Ideas, the necessity of truth, became *the* criterion of what counted as *logos*. If we have A and not-A, we face a contradiction, we do not have *a* proposition. But thanks to the principle of contradiction, one of the two must be true, and the other, necessarily false. On the problematological conception, when we face A or not-A, we have a problem, and the answer is, by definition, the elimination of the alternative. The contradiction consists of considering a question as an answer. The principle of contradiction must be then reinterpreted as a principle of answering, not of questioning. Otherwise, rhetoric and dialectic, where opposite standpoints are equally defended and asserted, would be impossible as *logos*. We can have a problem and be able to express it through what I have called "problematological answers", which reflect alternatives, even when these answers side on one of the two possible choices. "Apocritical" answers, on the other hand, resolve the alternatives. The principle of contradiction simply states that such a resolution cannot repeat and duplicate the alternative, and if it does, the alternative is to be considered as the expression of some question and not that of *the* solution. But this is not the way the founding fathers of propositionalism understood their supreme principle. For them, an alternative A/not-A is unacceptable to reason because it is a contradiction, that is an impossibility, and they never saw A versus not-A as a question. There is a necessity, and even a necessity of necessity, that is, A or not-A must necessarily be true, that is a proposition, and the other, not.

This model of Reason remained unchallenged until the fourteenth century, centered upon the solution and the necessity of eradicating alternatives as the meaning and intention of necessity. Even Descartes wanted apodictic truth and certainty. He reproached scholastic ontology to give rise to undecidable propositions, that is to doubtful and problematic assertions. God was on both sides, and truth, on neither one. As a result, a new foundation was required, in order to meet the emergency of apodicticity. It was the failure of his predecessors which, according to him, led him to find a new radical starting point. But if everything is doubtful, as Wittgenstein says, nothing can be asserted at all, not even that everything is doubtful. Hence, to say that one doubts is to say something which is undoubtful, it is to assert at least the very ideal of undoubtfulness as the ideal of answerhood to any possible doubt.[2]

But with Marx, Nietzsche and Freud, it appeared that there was no room left for a new starting point within the framework of Western propositionalism. And Derrida went further, by denying the possibility of any reconciliation between the foundationalist interrogation and a possible answer. The questioning process has no closure. We must face the problematic.

Problematology departs from deconstruction precisely at that moment. We must be able to speak of questions without abolishing them with our answers. The latter must be capable of expressing questions without referring to them as "traces" or "lacks" (of answers), as much as our answers must express what is solved inasmuch as it is solved. In order to express positively the question without reducing it to some answering, we must give room to a difference between the answers which express and maintain the questioning process, and those that close it upon some solution. Hence, the distinction between the problematological answers and the apocritical ones. We should stop seeing the problematic as the doubtful or as some obstacle, but rather as the starting point of thought. To formulate a question is a first step towards its solution, and not a hindrance. Within propositionalism, the deconstruction of propositionalism can only lead to *différance*, which is the internal movement of its own impossibilization coming to consciousness. But we should be more radical than deconstruction, and completely leave the realm of propositionalism. Derrida's thought invites us to do so.

Problematology is the answer to generalized problematicity. Instead of repressing it or seeing it as the own undoing of Western thought by itself, problematology takes questions seriously, for what they are. Its primary task may be seen negatively, if one wishes: if everything is hopelessly problematic, it becomes impossible to go beyond the realm of opinion, of competitive answers which represent only the perspectives of those who sustain them. But multiculturalism under the guise of philosophy is no philosophy at all: it is just the expression of different points of view, each as valuable as any other.

On the problematological view propounded here, the key concept is the problematological difference, that is the relationship between question and answer. There is no privileged, that is unquestioned and unquestionable, way of dealing with it. This difference can be made by the repression of questioning or by marking questions and answers syntactically or semantically in a different manner, if they come to be expressed. But the problematological difference can also be established by referring to questioning (and answering) explicitly, in the way *we* do it, when we thematize questioning as such. Western thought has always repressed questioning as such, granting its favor to answering, swallowing both of them into the indifference of the proposition. The efficiency of resolution came to be consecrated. But philosophy is better defined by rather saying it is radical questioning, even if philosophy has never questioned questioning so far. Now, such a task is inevitable, due to the collapse of all modes of propositionalist "answering", a collapse which has been labeled "the postmodern condition" by Lyotard.

At first, the return of the problematic has been characterized by a strong renewal of rhetoric. Derrida has contributed to such a renewal by showing[3] that it was impossible to draw a sharp dividing line between the literal and the figurative. It may explain Habermas' criticism, which stresses the impossibility of seeing a clear-cut difference in Derrida's analysis between the literal and the figurative, as if any language use were "poietic" in essence. We speak in order to mean something, and as a result, the literal must remain possible, and may not be swallowed into the figurative. Literality, which is necessary to language, cannot be reduced to a mere fiction. On the other hand, the rhetorical uses of language do not rest either on some pre-established truths that must be retrieved or unveiled, as if they existed by themselves, independently of their rhetorical phenomenalization.

How can we then explain the difference between the literal and the figurative? Their relationship is problematological: what is referred to in a given expression is no less, but no more, than the "what" itself. "Wh"-words refer to questions, not to things, even if such "wh"-words are those which enable us to single out what logicians have called the "reference" or the referential import in language. What is said, literally or not, refers to something in question, as the word "what" reminds us of it.

As to the figurative uses of language, they can be analyzed in the following way. If by the sentence 1) "It's cold", I mean 2) "I should wear a warm coat", we can say that 2) is the figurative meaning of 1), one among other possible readings of 1). We can also say that, by uttering 1), I raise some question that 2) answers. But if by 1), I only intended its literal reading, there would not be any question raised, because 1) would already be the answer. The meaning process would be closed by 1), while, if some other meaning is intended, 1) is merely problematological and the question of what 1) means would be raised by uttering 1).

The problematological conception of language[4] stresses the general relationship of sentences to the questions with respect to which they are the answers. That relationship is not always obvious, but it is none the less inherent in any language use. "Napoleon lost at Waterloo" embodies a chain of answers that the terms "Napoleon", "lost" or "Waterloo" embody as being unproblematic. Who is Napoleon, or where, when or what Waterloo, cease to be posed, but could be if necessary. "Napoleon" for instance, condensates the answers to those questions, as "Waterloo" does embody the answers to the aforementioned "wh"-questions. Hence also the semantic equivalence between "Napoleon lost at Waterloo" and

"Napoleon is the one *who* lost at Waterloo", for instance. In general, names represent answered questions that can be fully expressed if, referentially, what they refer to comes into question for some reason or other, such as the question concerning their meaning. Questioning is at work in literal meaning as well as in figurative reading, because questioning does not *have* to be referential. Questioning, as Wittgenstein put it in his *Philosophical Grammar*, is the first step when meaning is sought, and any answer will have to refer to that question, since it is raised as such. In brief, a literal reading is already an answer, but a figurative one is only a first step towards such an answer. From this, one cannot conclude that this latter answer is already there, as a hidden presence, to use Derrida's term. One has to find the answer, and what is literal is not anteriorily given. The erasure of questions by and in terms that solve them, such as "Napoleon" or "Waterloo", preclude figurative meaning, since the latter rests on questions that are raised, implicitly or formally, by some answer which thereby remains problematological. In "Richard is a lion", the question is raised by the metaphorical nature of the assertion, since Richard is said to be an animal and not an animal: to ascribe a metaphorical reading to this example is therefore a way of facing what would otherwise be a contradiction, and which is an alternative. In this case, we know it to be a worn metaphor, whose reading is codified by some essential feature of the lion, namely its courage. If I say, "Richard is a droplet", the enigma remains, due to the lack of that kind of pre-established answer.

The problematological difference can be interpreted as "being" what the Derridean *différance* becomes when we leave propositionalism, when questioning recovers a positivity which is excluded within the classical framework of ontotheology. Problematicity is historicity reflecting itself in the problems raised by the rhythm of history.

I am sure that Derrida would surely question such a view of thought, but thereby he would be questioning, and if he is questioning, his questioning would be a response, which would thereby reveal the primacy of the question–answer duality on which philosophy, any philosophy, also his own, rests.

University of Brussels

Notes

[1] In *Of Problematology*, University of Chicago Press, 1995.

[2] On this point, see my paper "The problematological conception of the *Cogito*", *Revue Internationale de Philosophie*, I, 1996, *Descartes*.

[3] In *Margins of Philosophy*, University of Chicago Press, 1982.

[4] As developed in *Rhetoric, Language and Reason*, Pennsylvania State University Press, 1994, Chs IV and V.

Chapter 2

The Delay of Consciousness

Daniel Giovannangeli

In 1967, *Of Grammatology* distinguishes the notion of "trace" from what is referred to by Jacques Derrida as the dialectic of retention and protention. Husserl's concept of temporality rests, indeed, incapable of understanding an experience that does not maintain an immediately preceding present:

> It is the problem of the deferred effect *(nachträglich)* of which Freud speaks. The temporality to which he refers cannot be that lends itself to a phenomenology of consciousness of presence.[1]

What sense would it make to speak of an unconscious temporality? And in the work of Derrida, does this apparent taking over of the temporality of consciousness by another temporality coincide with a pure abandoning, simple, brutal and definite, of phenomenology?

Determining the unconscious processes as intemporal, was this not for Freud a way of withdrawing them by fiat from the jurisdiction of philosophy? The opening lines of *Beyond the Pleasure Principle* ironically underline the vanity of philosophical analyses of pleasure and displeasure.[2] But though the essence of pleasure and of displeasure seems entirely phenomenal, the question of the possibility of an unconscious effect does indeed arise.[3] To this question of *Metapsychology*, the responses diverge: when Michel Henry uses his theory to preserve the phenomenology of pure affection, Jean-Francois Lyotard is driven by the Freudian question to complicate the structure of phenomenological temporality.

In *Beyond the Pleasure Principle*, Freud comes across a problem which, he suggests, should be treated in depth. It is advisable to confront the intemporality of physical processes with a Kantian thesis (which Freud warns, would then be strongly shaken) that is, the thesis which reckons time among our "necessary forms of thought".[4] The phrasing stays fast and allusive; it seems to substitute thought for sensitivity and to possibly overlook the rigorously transcendental bearing of Kant's aesthetics. But whereas the question is merely outlined by Freud, Derrida has managed to come to grips with it on several occasions. Where he recalls it most strongly, in *Freud and the Scene of Writing*, it is through a double gesture, a gesture for displacing it. It first detaches Freud's concept of a "supplementary delay" from the traditional framework of reminiscence, philosophical reminiscence (from Plato to Hegel) as well as literary reminiscence (Proust). Calling to mind the Wolfman and quoting from the passage of *L'Esquisse* relative to repression in hysteria, he realizes that the past present is not revived, but is, in some sort, produced in its truth. However, though the unconscious processes remain immeasurable to reminiscence, Derrida refuses to jump to the conclusion that these processes shy away from all philosophical determinations of time:

> The timelessness of the unconscious is no doubt determined only in opposition to a common concept of time, the traditional concept, the metaphysical concept : the time of mechanics or the time of consciousness. We ought perhaps to read Freud the way Heidegger read Kant: like the Cogito, unconscious is no doubt timeless only from the standpoint of a certain vulgar conception of time.[5]

The same reflection re-emerges in Derrida's commentary of *Beyond the Pleasure Principle*. In this, Derrida proposes indeed to bring Freud's temporality back to the "auto-affective structure of time (that which there gives itself to receive is no present being as) such as it is described in Husserl's '*Lectures on internal consciousness of time*' or Heidegger's '*Kantbuch*'".[6] This is to say that the gap Freud sets up between Kant's philosophy and his own would call for a philosophical reconsideration, at least from the standpoint of the phenomenological determinations of temporality which are philosophically original. In as much as temporality frees itself from the primacy of the present-being, is it not the case that phenomenological temporality paves the way toward another figure of time, whose specificity would warrant the idea of a temporality of the unconscious? If so, the rejection of a temporality of the unconscious would only hold against the vulgar conception of time which Husserl and Heidegger (following in the footsteps of a Kant that Freud allegedly ignored) have precisely liberated philosophy from.

Jacques Derrida recognized the debt that he contracted *vis-à-vis* the phenomenological conception of time. His Forward to the 1990 edition, of his paper of 1953–1954, *Le Problème de la genèse dans la philosophie de Husserl*, indicates the important role played there by Husserl's interpretation of time in a dialectic perspective. The appeal to the dialectic is intended to surmount the obstacle that the irreducibility of the constituted time puts in the way of the research of a constituting origin of time. Derrida raises this difficulty, which entails retentional and protentional modifications for Husserl's conception of inherent impression. In spite of the overtly expressed intention of Husserl, did these not lead him to renounce a principle of inherent impression? They lead at least to a recognition that the inherent present itself is already constituted, that the phenomenological present "is not pure and appears pure to itself only in so far as it is the outcome of a genetic composition".[7] In Lecture § 3 of 1905, Husserl takes the description of melody to have something to teach us for a phenomenology of time. He remarked that just as a symphony cannot permit, on pain of destroying itself, that the appearance of a sound should trigger the disappearing of its precedent, a symphony cannot permit either, except to merge with a genuine cacophony, that all the past sounds be kept without modification in the actual consciousness. The question then should arise whether the necessity of the retentional and protentional modification stays compatible with the inherentness of impression. In § 31, Husserl tried hard to keep the latter pure of all modification in conferring upon it the status of a "non-modified absolute".[8] However, he dismissed almost immediately, in § 32, the eventuality of a "*now* that nothing has preceded".[9] Does this not impede the value of the inherentness of present impressions? If no present can be, unless constituted, and if every present stays inseparable from the immediate past that it keeps, does not the idea of a paradoxical inherent delay of consciousness compel recognition? Husserl explicitly disallowed this in § 13, and judged phenomenologically inconceivable the empirical point of view that allows or at least contemplates the possibility of "an initial consciousness, that begins by a recent memory, without there having been a preliminary perception".[10] On the contrary, *Le Problème de la genèse* takes on, at the same time, the risk of adulterating the transcendental purity by bringing in empirical ingredients and the remote possibility, discarded by Husserl, of an inherent delay of consciousness. The solution that Derrida puts forth in his first work falls within the scope of phenomenological ontology. Sharing Husserl's contention that the instant of inherent impression already supposes retention would amount to introducing both the anteriority and the transcendence of a thing constituted into the heart of the constituent consciousness. Husserl may well claim to stick to the thesis of the purity of the constituent origin of time. If in practice he could not prevent the return of the constituted in the constituent, "phenomenology may no more be absolutely the master of its house. Ontology may already be in its place."[11] Ignoring the superficial distinction between the subject and the world which belongs to the level of the constituted, "what essential difference is there between the transcendence of the constituted moments within the pure flux experienced in relation to an inherent 'now' and the transcendence of 'real' objectivities of time?"[12] Moreover, as Husserl himself notes in a passage from *Lectures* that captured Maurice Merleau-Ponty's attention before Michel Henry's,[13] reflection introduces a splitting in two that forbids the coincidence between the constituent and the constituted: "That [which] in the instantaneous actuality of the flux [of] consciousness is caused to appear, that is a past phase of this same flux in the succession of these retentional movements."[14] In this entanglement between the constituent and the constituted, Derrida in a way detected the force of an internal necessity which pushes phenomenology to open up to ontology, instead of suspending the latter as it was intended to. The retention of the past would then refer back to the facticity of the world. A common antecedence would impose on the consciousness both the world and the past that it retains. In other words, the constitution would depend on the given that it retains while overtaking it.

> When Husserl recognizes an *apriori* necessity of the antecedence of an impression to all retention and that, on the other hand, he maintains that the present retention originally exhibits a character of intentional evidence, is he not introducing, under the form of "datum hylétique", passively received, the transcendent object that he contends to exclude from his analysis ?[15]

The delay *in* the consciousness is, otherwise said, inseparable from the delay *of* consciousness with respect to the being as such.

How could we fail to notice that this interpretation of delay in terms of phenomenological ontology appears to espouse and even ground afresh the movement of Sartreian thought? Starting from Husserl, but also moving against him, *The Transcendence of the Ego* adopts the thesis of an impersonal spontaneity, albeit individual, of consciousness. In his essay, Sartre pushes to the extreme the importance of transverse intentionality that radiates Husserl's *Lectures*.

> Indeed consciousness is defined by intentionality. By intentionality consciousness transcends itself. It unifies itself by escaping from itself ... The object is transcendent to the consciousness which grasps, and it is in the object that the unity of the consciousness is found. It will be said that a principle of unity "within duration" is nonetheless needed if the continual flux of consciousness is to be [capable of] positing transcendent objects outside the flux. Consciousness must be perpetual syntheses of past and present consciousness. This is correct. But it is characteristic that Husserl, who studied the subjective unification of consciousness in The Internal Consciousnes of Time – (in German in English trans.) – never had recourse to a synthetic power of the I. It is consciousness which unifies itself, concretely, by a play of "transversal" intentionalities which are concrete and real retentions of past consciousness. Thus consciousness refers perpetually to itself. Whoever says "a consciousness" says the "whole of consciousness", and this singular property belongs to consciousness itself, aside from whatever relations it may have to the I.[16]

Later, *Being and Nothingness* bluntly returns Husserl's temporality to idealism and even to instantaneism. The ontology of *Being and Nothingness* corrected Husserl's intentionality by assuming that "consciousness implies in it's being a non-conscious and transphenomenal being".[17] It is remarkable that in limiting to the past that which was extended to temporality itself by the *Carnets de la drôle de guerre* still involved in separating the essence of consciousness, of contingency, from one's temporal being, Sartre is prone to identify the past of consciousness with the facticity of being. *Les Carnets* remarks that, "our temporality and our facticity are one and the same thing".[18] Being in itself is that which *Being and Nothingness* identifies facticity with, before drawing the conclusion, also drawn by Derida, that – to simplify a lot – "facticity and 'past' are two words denoting one and the same thing".[19]

Notwithstanding, the breach brought out by *Transcendence of the Ego* has not escaped Jacques Derrida. The introduction to the *Origin of Geometry*, defines writing as a transcendental field without subject:[20] to the extent to which it virtualizes the dialogue, writing forges a sort of transcendental field which the subject can leave. It is worth noting, however, that though the initial version of *Of Grammatology* published in 1966 carries the theme about writing in an explicitly transcendental perspective – writing is referred to as the "transcendental condition of all linguistic systems"[21] – the book in 1967 erases this reference to the transcendental and transforms the passage into a "condition of all linguistic systems".[22] In spite of this closeness to Sartre and to the latter's move towards the deepening of the ontology of phenomenology, it is in resolutely Heideggerian[23] terms that an ontology is marked out by Derrida. More precisely, *Le Problème de la genèse dans la philosophie de Husserl* accedes to the demand of an "ontological dialectic of time".[24] Giving a radical turn to the dialectic interpretations put forward by Cavailles and Tran-Duc-Thao, Derrida makes the hypothesis that it is "possible to found – in its ontological possibility and sense (together) – an absolute dialectic from the dialectic and the non-dialectic".[25] Without apparent rupture on this point, the introduction to the *Origin of Geometry* continues to invoke a dialectic of retention and protention referred to as the dialectic between the dialectical with the non-dialectical; like "the dialectic between the dialectical (the indefinite mutual and irreducible implication of protentions and retentions) and the non-dialectical (the absolute and concrete identity of the Living Present, the universal form of all consciousness".[26]

With *La Voix et le phénomène* in 1967, the shift from the dialectic to the *différance* comes about visibly. When he envisions temporality from the standpoint of "the identity between the identity and non-identity", and "the difference in auto-affection", Derrida wonders whether "this dialectic (to all the senses of this word and before all speculative resumption of this concept) does not open the living to the différance".[27] It is this perspective that consumes the rupture with the dialectic. The lecture of January 1968 on "The differance", restores precisely Freud's *Nachträglichkeit* in conjunction with the idea borrowed from Levinas, of a past which never was present:

> The structure of delay (*Nachträglichkeit*) prohibits in effect, that one reduces temporalization (temporization) to a simple dialectic complication of the Living Present as inherent and incessant synthesis, constantly renewing to onself above oneself gathered, gathering of retentional traces of protentional works.[28]

La Voix et le phénomène clears, in effect, the obstacle erected in front of the phenomenological, by the possibility of an inherent delay. Derrida emphasizes the way in which Husserl, in the Supplement IX of the *Lectures*, denied himself the right of linking retention to the conscious: "Speaking of an 'unconscious' content which would become conscious only later on (*nachträglich*) is an unquestionable absurdity. Consciousness is necessarily conscious-being in all of its phases."[29] Michel Henry praised the clairvoyance of Husserl, who steps back here when confronted to the modifications and who worries about the weight that he imparts to the past. Derrida's lecture underlines the rigorous necessity which leads Husserl, unwillingly, up to the *Nachträglichkeit*:

> This is not a coincidence if the *Lectures* on the intimate consciousness of time confirms the dominance of the present and on the same occasion rejects the "after-shock" of the conscious – becoming an "unconscious content", i.e. the structure of temporality implied by all the texts of Freud.[30]

Though Derrida acquieses to this necessity which Husserl resists, if he follows in the footsteps of Freud, the question for him – to switch from one author to the other – does not arise. The complex structure that "produces a delay to what it is said to be added",[31] is not rigorously answerable to the pure and simple opposition of consciousness and the unconscious. It cannot be completely exhausted by referring to the ontology of the present. Admittedly the latter requires this opposition, but it does from within philosophy:

> Moreover, there is not any possible objection within philosophy, concerning this privilege of the present-now. This privilege defines the element itself of philosophical thought, it is the *evidence* itself, the conscious thought itself. It commands all possible concepts of truth and sense. One cannot suspect it without beginning to enucleate the consciousness itself from a standpoint outside philosophy which deprives discourse of all security and all possible foundation. And it is the privilege of the actual present which is the pivot around which develops – in ultimate instance – this debate, which cannot ressemble any other debate, between philosophy that is always the philosophy of the presence, and a thought of the non-presence, that is not inevitably its opposite, nor necessarily a mediation of the negative absence, nor even a theory of the non-presence *qua* unconscious.[32]

The anachrony of the *Nachträglichkeit* borders and overflows philosophy. Its strange temporality points out from outside of philosophy the anachrony of time itself, which is somehow the condition of phenomenological time.[33]

Notes

* Translated by Patricia Connolly (University of Liège, Loyota University MA).

[1] J. Derrida, *Of Grammatology*, Engl. trans. Spivak, Johns Hopkins Press, 1976, p. 67.

[2] S. Freud, *Beyond the Pleasure Principle*, Engl. trans. Strachey, W.W. Norton and Company, New York, 1961, p. 25. Commentary of Jacques Derrida, *The Postcard: From Socrates to Freud and Beyond*, Engl. trans. A. Bass, University of Chicago Press, Illinois, 1978, p. 234.

[3] S. Freud, *Metapsychology*, trans. Fr. J. Laplanche and J.B. Pontalis, Gallimard, Folio-Essais, 1986, pp. 82-83. Commentary of M. Henry, *Généalogie de la psychanalyse*, P.U.F., 1985, p. 368 and sv.; of J.F. Lyotard, *Heidegger and "The Jews"*, Engl. trans. J.P. Leavey, University of Nebraska Press, Nebraska, 1978, p. 31 and sv., "Emma", *Nouvelle revue de psychanalyse*, 1989 (39), pp. 51 and sv.

[4] S. Freud, *Beyond the Pleasure Principle*, op. cit., p. 31. Commentary of J.F. Lyotard, *Discours, figure*, Klincksieck, 1971, pp. 152-153 and p. 337; of P.L. Assoun, *Freud, la philosophie et les philosophes*, P.U.F.,1976, pp. 159 and sv.

[5] J. Derrida, *Writing and Difference*, Engl. trans. Alan Bass, University of Chicago Press, 1978, p. 215.

[6] *Postcards*, op. cit., p. 359.

[7] J. Derrida, *Of Grammatology*, Engl. trans. Spivak, Johns Hopkins Press, 1976, p. 67.
[8] E. Husserl, *Leçons pour une phénoménologie de la conscience intime du temps*, trad. fr. H. Dussort, P.U.F., 1964, p. 88.
[9] E. Husserl, ibid., p. 91.
[10] E. Husserl, ibid., p. 48.
[11] *Le Problème de la genèse*, op. cit., p. 117.
[12] Ibid., p. 111.
[13] I allow myself to refer to my study "Effect and Phenomenon. Remarks on the 'Hyletic' Phenomenology" in *La Voix des phénomènes*, Publication of the Saint-Louis University Faculty, Brussels, 1997, pp. 319-330.
[14] E. Husserl, *Leçons*, op. cit., p. 109.
[15] *Le Problème de la genèse*, op. cit., p. 121.
[16] J.P. Sartre, *The Transcendence of the Ego*, Engl. trans. Forest Williams and Robert Kirkpatrick, Hill and Wang, NY, 1978, pp. 38-39.
[17] J.P. Sartre, *Being and Nothingness*, Engl. trans. H.E. Barnes, Washington Square Press, New York, 1956, pp. 23-24.
[18] J.P. Sartre, *Carnets de la drôle de guerre*, Gallimard, 2nd edn, 1995, p. 438.
[19] J.P. Sartre, *Being and Nothingness*, op. cit., p. 173.
[20] J. Derrida, Introduction to the *Origin of Geometry*, Engl. trans. John P. Leavey Jr., University of Nebraska Press, Lincoln Nebraska, 1978, p. 80.
[21] J. Derrida, "De la grammatologie, II" in *Critique*, January 1966 (224), p. 31.
[22] *Of Grammatology*, op. cit., p. 60.
[23] *Le Problème de la genèse*, p. ex., pp. 30, 67, 120, 196-197, 226.
[24] Ibid., p. 209.
[25] Ibid., p. 17.
[26] Introduction to the *Origin of Geometry*, op. cit., p. 143.
[27] J. Derrida, *La Voix et le phénomène*, P.U.F., 1967, p. 77.
[28] J. Derrida, *Marges de la philosophie*, Minuit, 1972, pp. 21-22.
[29] E. Husserl, *Leçons*, op. cit., p. 160. Commentary of M. Henry, *Phénoménologie matérielle*, P.U.F., 1990, p. 52.
[30] *La Voix et le phénomène*, op. cit., pp. 70-71.
[31] Ibid., p. 99.
[32] Ibid., p. 70.
[33] Jacques Derrida speaks now of "time before time", of "anachronic time", of "anachrony of time itself", in "Ouvertures", in the prefatory remarks to the commentary of *Timée* by S. Margel, *Le Tombeau du dieu artisan*, Minuit, 1995.

Bibliography of English Sources

Derrida, Jacques: *Of Grammatology*. Translated by Gayatri Chakravorty Spivak, Johns Hopkins Press; Baltimore, Maryland, 1976.

Derrida, Jacques: *The Postcard: From Socrates to Freud and Beyond*. Translated by Alan Bass, University of Chicago Press; Chicago, Illinois, 1987.

Derrida, Jacques: *Writing and Difference*. Translated by Alan Bass, University of Chicago Press; Chicago, Illinois, 1978.

Freud, Sigmund: *Beyond the Pleasure Principle*. Translated by James Strachey, W.W. Norton and Company; New York, 1961.
Husserl, Edmund: *Origin of Geometry*. Translated by John P. Leavey Jr., University of Nebraska Press; Lincoln, Nebraska, 1978.
Lyotard, Jean-Francois: *Heidegger and "The Jews"*. Translated by Andreas Michel and Mark Roberts, University of Minnesota Press; Minneapolis, Minnesota, 1990.
Sartre, Jean-Paul: *Being and Nothingness*. Translated by Hazel E. Barnes, Washington Square Press; New York, 1956.
Sartre, Jean-Paul: *The Transcendence of the Ego*. Translated by Forrest Williams and Robert Kirkpatrick, Hill and Wang; New York, 1960.

Chapter 3

The Decision of Analogy:
A Remark on Derrida, Reader of Plato

Karel Thein

On page 159 of "Plato's Pharmacy"[1] is imprinted the following paragraph:

> Plato often uses the example of letters of the alphabet in order to come to grips with a problem. They give him a better grip of things; that is, he can use them to explain dialectics – but he never 'comes to grip with' the writing he uses. His intentions are always apparently didactic and analogical. But they conform to a constant necessity, which is never thematized as such: it always serves to make apparent the law of difference, the irreducibility of structure and relation, of proportionality, of analogy.

The present article is nothing but concise commentary on the second part of this paragraph, which seems to express something decisive concerning Plato's dialogues as well as Derrida's Plato. For in the texts like "Plato's Pharmacy" or *Khôra*, the analogy does not simply become an object of analysis, but keeps its quality of a bond of terms that cannot be reduced to any common denominator nor be subsumed under one genus. The analogy is rather actively engaged. Yet this operation of analogy certainly does not limit itself solely to the two above-mentioned texts. In a certain way, this *mise en œuvre* or operation of analogy marks Derrida's undertaking as a whole, which it is not easy to name. To this lack of a generic name – what is at stake here is not some philosophical genre, be it a new or an ancient one – corresponds, according to Derrida, an open chain of names to which "writing", "trace", "différance", supplement", pharmakon", and even "deconstruction" all belong by the same right, and not as a series of examples.[2] In a passage from *Positions*, these names are identified as so many marks, as certain marks "que j'ai appelés *par analogie* (je le souligne) des indécidables".[3] Apparently, Derrida himself underscores in this way the expression "by analogy" for two reasons. First, it is because these indecidables involve the text in a tension without resolution, a tension that undermines or disorganizes any possibility of sense which would be more general,[4] and second, because the same thing is true about these marks themselves (they do not form any meta-text): just as the texts they haunt, the indecidables cannot be subsumed under the unity of a common genre, and this is why they can be given one and the same name ("indécidables") only "by analogy".[5] And if the indecidable calls for a decision and if one decides only against the indecidable,[6] we should ask a question concerning the decision of analogy as such, the decision that entails the elaboration of analogy or emersion of analogy as a form or a figure of discourse.

Derrida comes to this question in various texts, be it with respect to Aristotle, Condillac or Kant, Husserl or Lévinas. In these texts, the analogy as a relation of proportionality is called in question through an inquiry into its source in the *logos*, and is understood as an operation which goes beyond the terms it sets in order. Here is just one example, born out of the reading of the *Critique of Judgement*:

> L'analogie entre la productivité libre de la nature et la productivité libre du génie, entre Dieu et le Poète, n'est pas seulement un rapport de proportionnalité ou un rapport entre deux – deux sujets, deux origines, deux productions. Le procès analogique est aussi une remontée vers le *logos*. L'origine est le *logos*. L'origine de l'analogie, ce dont procède et vers quoi fait retour l'analogie, c'est le *logos*, raison et parole, source comme bouche et embouchure.[7]

The figuring out of analogy would then be, at least partially, tied up to what indicates the very structure of this composed name, where *ana* derives from *anô*, "upwards".[8] Yet if we pay attention to this determination, it may be first of all thanks to the analogy born in the dialogues of Plato, more exactly in book VI of the *Republic*: the analogy of good and sun. If this precise analogy seems to have influenced the very notion of analogy, it is nevertheless far from being the only one which, in the dialogues, comes out from the movement of *logos*.

First, we should take note of the fact that all three moments to which Derrida as a reader of Plato has been paying attention undoubtedly most often – the *pharmakon*, *khora* of the *Timaeus*, the *epekeina tés ousias* of the *Republic* – have, notwithstanding their mutual heterogeneity, something to do precisely with the question of analogy and of the role it plays not in this or that particular teaching or doctrine, but in the philosophical performance as an exercise which has to create its own ground. As far as the *pharmakon* is concerned, the analogy proportions the *pharmaka* to the *logoi*, with all the consequences for the difference between the good and the bad art of writing. In a completely different way, the discourse of Timaeus on what he calls *khôra*, the discourse he announces as a brand new kind of explanation (48b5-6), is deeply embedded in the analogy of four elements that do form the body of the world if not its soul. Timaeus' dream touches upon the generation of the very terms of a great analogy that sustains the *kosmos*.[9] Finally, the analogy of good and sun (a sketch that serves as a substitute for the discourse about the good as the ultimate producing cause responsible for what is and the knowledge of what is) maintains without resolution the tension between analogy and genealogy which cross each other in the text of the *Republic*. The tension between these two poles reminds us that in the dialogues, the reasoning by analogy belongs to the most different strata or levels of sense, ranging from the elements up to the whole of the *kosmos*, so that the moment of passage from one level to another does not depend on any uniform grid, but marks rather the creation or elaboration of analogy as such. With this creation, however, Plato's dialogues entertain the most ambiguous relations. If the figure of analogy is not a Platonic invention, but originates in the wake of Homeric comparisons and expands its field in Empedocles or in the Hippocratic writings, it does not form a peacefully possessed heritage. The second sailing of Plato's Socrates, his inquiry into the soul and the "ideas", goes directly against the analogical schemes born out of the *historia peri phuseôs*, the inquiry into the nature that includes the nature of man, who is seen as composed of the same elements as the rest of physical world.[10] The return of analogy in the dialogues constitutes the ground for Socrates' confrontation with the pre-Socratism of his interlocutors and the pre-Socratism somehow present in his own philosophizing.[11] It is this return, chiefly that of book VI of the *Republic* – where Socrates elaborates a brand new and philosophically constitutive analogy – which will play a decisive role in the future adventures of philosophy, adventures launched by Aristotle and misreadings of Aristotle on the one hand, and by Neoplatonic misreadings of Plato on the other. Should I adventure far beyond my subject to confront just once the history of philosophy with a metaphysical determination, I would say that the thinking of analogy, and hence of the equivocity of being, plays throughout this history a role as important and ambivalent as the "metaphysics of presence". Both of them, however, become accomplices only when the metaphysics of degrees of being starts to substitute, in the course of the history, for the different senses of being.[12] It would be interesting to follow this movement that makes the analogy ascend from the pagan authors up to the analogy between the creator and his creation.[13] More modestly, and because of a necessary economy, I shall limit myself in these pages to a single analogy which sets to work the *pharmakon*, the one precisely which Derrida calls "by analogy" indecidable. This *pharmakon* repeats and inscribes itself in a Platonic intrigue which begins already before Plato.

First of all, it is important to specify once again that, in the dialogues, the way of analogy and the way of dialectics – the beautiful way as a gift of the gods Socrates speaks about in the *Philebus* – do not coincide but complement each other as different ways to determine or lay down the very *objet* of a philosophical inquiry. What is apprehended and set in order through an analogical bond is not the same "something" that becomes directly an *objet* of the question *ti esti*. According to Derrida as a reader of Plato, the form of the question "what is?" is "produced by the very thing it questions".[14] According to Plato, the horizon of this production depends on the presence of a determinable *ti*, which has the power to affect something or to be affected, and which precedes and determines in its turn what can be *ontôs* (cf. *Sophist* 247d8–e4). The form and the determination of form of the Socratic questioning do not exactly overlap, and it is perhaps because of this difference that to explain dialectics demands exposure of the analogy, even if this exposure leads to its dismissal. If then in "Plato's Pharmacy", just as later in *Khôra*, the analogical bond plays an important role, it is in no way a casual feature: the analogy marks the limits of the competence of *ti esti*, but at the same time it produces a different philosophical competence. From this point of view, Derrida's reading of Plato recalls first of all to our memory that in the movement of *logos*, the analogy is never simply already given, but has to be created,[15] and that this creation depends upon a decision taken against the indecidable which precedes any polarity of the two, and then four, terms ordered in proportional and mutually equal bipolar relations (*analogia* defined as *isotés logôn*). It is precisely this "store of deep background", this undecided shadow of any already discriminated difference, that Derrida, according to his own decision, calls *pharmacy*.[16]

From page 111/127, "Plato's Pharmacy" deals with the writing as *pharmakon* which produces the play of the relations between the philosophy, the rhetoric, the sophistic (112/128). It deals with the *logos* already translated in the writing and with the writing already translated in the judgement, with the immutability of the law whose graphic imprint makes it withdraw from the movement of *phusis* (cf. 113/129), and with the graphic imprint transformed into the possible model of science, *epistémé*, which by the way presupposes the distinction between the voice and the articulated speech as a mark of *anthrôpos*. In these pages, the threshold of a pre-Socratic decision of Gorgias and of a decision of Plato's Socrates is being approached. We wake up in what Derrida calls "the ambivalent, indeterminate space of the *pharmakon*" (115/131). The resources of this "space" will then allow the two different blames of the writing to partake in the deeper possibility of a praise of the writing, insofar as what is oral and what is written partake in the same structure of the *logos* as such and do not differ, except through the efficiency of their action: what is said and is written coincide even where "to speak" and "to write" separate from each other, and only the inverted commas will later come to trace this separation, at least temporarily.[17] On the level of the body, the spoken *logos* is then not superior to the *grammata* in its being, but only as a human *praxis*, and even this superiority is only partial and conditioned. On the other hand, the *grammata* seem to be superior in their being thanks to the exactness of their combination that makes them intelligible. If the consonants and the soundless do not contain but a small part of the unlimited – this unlimited which is the matter of the *phôné* – the vowels (*phôneenta*) can then function as a variable bond (*desmos*) of the articulated speech.[18] On the whole, it belongs always to the letters and never to the voice to supply the science with a *paradeigma*, because the voice is not learnt but given at the birth together with the body which at first grows and then diminishes. The voice is too natural, and this is why it is ambiguous: the voice flows, just as the light of the *Republic* (508b6-7). Both the voice and the letters touch upon the limits of sense, but they touch upon its opposed limits. As units that divide a continuum, the letters are co-original with the dialectics. The *grammata* articulate the *phôné* and make it possible to say or to write "something". The *grammata* are forgotten at the moment of any individual's birth, and yet they are always in the soul as a condition of its capacity to recall everything it has experienced both on this earth and in Hades.[19] The praise of writing is always already set in order, its blame is self-contradictory.

What Derrida underscores in this moment is, then, precisely the contrast between the Socrates of the *Phaedrus* and the orators as far as their *condemnation* of writing is concerned. In both case, the *grammata* seem inferior to the speech, but the declared structure of this inferiority is each time a different one. On the side of the orators, "if the written word is scorned, it is not as a *pharmakon* coming to corrupt memory and truth. It is because *logos* is a more effective *pharmakon*".[20] This *logos* that Gorgias calls *pharmakon* is in its efficiency ambivalent because it can be good or bad, and its power, its *dunamis*, precedes the very separation of the "good" and the "bad". The difference between the Socrates of the *Phaedrus* and Gorgias becomes apparent on the grounds of recognition of the ambivalence or indetermination of *logos*: it is on the grounds of this recognized ambivalence that Gorgias decides about the determination of the good over the falsehood or the lie. In his *Encomium of Helen*, quoted several times by Derrida, "Gorgias indicts *logos* in its capacity to lie".[21] To tame this power, Gorgias wishes "to introduce some reasoning (*logismos*) into speech (*logos*)".[22] The decision of Gorgias is to let the *logismos* act upon the *logos*, and it is in this way that he "*determines* truth as a *world*, a structure or order, the counterpart (*kosmos*) of *logos*". It is precisely in doing so, adds Derrida, that "he no doubt prefigures the Platonic gesture".[23] These sentences of Derrida remind us the beginning of *Encomium of Helen*: "The order (*kosmos*) of a city is excellence of its citizens, of a body beauty, of a soul wisdom, of an action virtue, of a discourse truth".[24] Opposing the instances of *kosmos* to the *akosmia*, Gorgias sets up what the *kosmos* does consist in through a series of relations belonging to different levels, and it is this series that seems to provide the matrix for the action of *logos* whose power is then determined as persuasion. This persuasion is described in its functioning or technique, praised as something divine (§§ 6–13), and finally resumed in the *Encomion*'s paragraph 14, quoted and commented upon by Derrida on the next page of his text:[25]

> The power of speech (*tou logou dunamis*) is in the same relation (*ton auton de logon*) to the disposition of the soul (*pros tén tés psuchés taxin*) as the disposition of the drugs (*tôn pharmakôn taxin*) to the nature of bodies (*tén tôn sômatôn phusin*). For just as certain drugs evacuate certain humours from the bodies, each that akin to itself, and some bring an end to disease and others to life, so also certain speeches distress, others delight, certain cause fear, others make the hearers bold; others drug and bewitch the soul with a kind of evil persuasion (*tén psuchén epharmakeusan kai exegoeteusan*).

If some of the speeches drug and bewitch the soul, it is because, according to Gorgias, *goéteia kai mageia*, sorcery and witchcraft, are the "double arts", *dissoi technai*, whose ambivalence seems to reflect the divine origin of that persuasive *logos* which pervades the soul and transforms its opinions, these opinions which substitute for the knowledge about the things of the past, the present and the future.[26] The *pharmakon* of speech operates then in between the memory and the oracle – the two divine dimensions of time – and the enchantment caused by this *pharmakon* substitutes for an inquiry made about the present itself.[27] The change of a present state of soul replaces the possibility to apprehend any present state which could be identified as such, and we can only recollect the Hippocratic definition of *pharmakon*: "*pharmaka* are all [things] which change the present state (*to pareon*); and all [things] which are strong enough introduce a change".[28] This reminder of Hippocrates justifies also by the fact that the action of *pharmaka* on the humours, mentioned in Gorgias' text quoted by Derrida, seems very closely related to the one described in the Hippocratic treatise *On the Nature of Man*:

> For when the *pharmakon* enters the body, it first withdraws that humour of the body which is most akin to itself, and then it draws and purges the other humours. For just as (*hôs gar*) things that are sown and grow in the earth, when they enter it, draw each that constituent of the earth which is nearest akin to it ... such too is the action of *pharmaka* in the body (*toiouton de ti kai ta pharmaka poiei en tôi sômati*). Those that withdraw bile first evacuate absolutely pure bile, then bile that is mixed; those that withdraw phlegm first withdraw absolutely pure phlegm, and then phlegm that is mixed.[29]

In this passage, the analogy is as evident as in the *Encomion of Helen*. The difference between these texts consists first in the content of one of the two proportions, and then in the fact that the Hippocratic author explains the action of *pharmakon* while Gorgias makes use of this action to explain in his turn the action of *logos*. Apparently, Gorgias conserves from the Hippocratic analogy one relation (that of the *pharmakon* to the body) and replaces the other (that of the things sown or vegetals to the earth) by the relation between the discourse and the soul. The most evident consequence of this move is the redoubling of sense of the word *logos* upon which Derrida draws our attention:

> the relation (the analogy) between the *logos*/soul relation and the *pharmakon*/body relation is itself designated by the term *logos*. The name of the relation is the same as that of one of its terms. The *pharmakon* is *comprehended* in the structure of *logos*. This comprehension is both a *domination* and a *decision*.[30]

This short commentary of § 14 of *Encomion of Helen* yields to two different readings. According to the first one, Derrida would just describe the act of inscription of the *logos* in a relation, of inscription that passes through the lexical ambiguity or homonymy of the word *logos*: the *logos* in the sense of "relation" corresponds apparently to the *logismos* that Gorgias decides to introduce in the *logos* as discourse or speech. The proportioning is the ordering or arrangement, the act of producing of the *kosmos* that the rhetoric wants to guarantee. The second reading does not deny the precedent one, but goes beyond the level of a lexical ambiguity: the double function or structure of the name *logos* would not be a simple homonymy, but rather an opening of the possibility that not only one proportion of two terms within an analogy concerns the *pharmaka*, but that the whole analogy with its four terms becomes in its turn a kind of *pharmakon*. For Gorgias does not say that the *logos* is more or less like *pharmakon*, but maintains that it is with the *logos* as with the *pharmakon*. The double sense of the word *logos* would be itself a part of the magic of discourse, which does not lend itself to an univocal apprehension, but is liable to transformations into the bad as well as good persuasion. This second reading seems to foreshadow what Derrida as reader of Plato is interested in, that is the difficulty to discriminate between the socratic and the sophistic *logos*. In the next pages of his text, having analyzed some passages from the dialogues where Socrates runs the risk of being arrested as a sorcerer or enchanter, like *goés* or *pharmakeus*, Derrida questions indeed what he calls "this *analogy* that ceaselessly refers the socratic *pharmakon* to the sophistic *pharmakon* and, proportioning them to each other, makes us go back indefinitely from one to the other".[31]

Is it here that Gorgias' analogy becomes itself a magical *pharmakon* used equally by the Sophist and by Socrates, for the same purpose of changing the present state of soul of their interlocutors? Socrates himself, with all his irony, appears as sophist (*Sophist* 268b1-4), and may be distinguished only through his strategical position. Yet Socrates' strategy consists in denying its own strategical character, which is emphasized by the repeated use of the shortest possible question *ti esti*: to always say the same things about the same things is divinely sublime but humanly idiotic, and the philosophy partakes of both. At this occasion, one understands the importance of the fact that the syntagm "to say (or think) always the same things about the same things" belongs in Plato not only to the activity of Socrates (*Gorgias* 490e9–10) and to the writing (*Phaedrus* 275d9), but also to the divine thought of the stars (*Timaeus* 40a9–b1). Socratic irony, the irony of dialogues, overturns each time the preceding discourse without changing one single letter of it, because Socrates himself has nothing to say. The irony of this Socrates who does not write, the irony that, in the dialogue, substitutes for the difference between oral and written, does not reverse the content, but the terms and so the power of Sophistic *logos*. According to Derrida, it is in this ironic overturning that "science and death" are at stake.[32] Yet if death concerns man but not the human experience of *logos* (*Philebus* 15d4–8), and if the science or knowledge that has to be iterable and reproducible assumes the role of *pharmakon* (*Critias* 106b5–6), then their relation may – still according to Derrida – be resumed in a following way: the science is to death what the well-written *logos* is to badly-written *logos*. This new analogy is justified by the passages on writing in the *Phaedrus*, which are apparently not without relation to the above-quoted texts of Gorgias and (so-called) Hippocrates. Hence the necessity to examine the exact nature of the bond that ties the more ancient analogies of Gorgias and Hippocrates to this new analogy of well-written *logos* and science on the one hand, and badly-written *logos* and death on the other.

If we can clearly see that Gorgias' text on speech and *pharmakon* makes use of the Hippocratic analogy of what is sown in the earth and the *pharmakon* which enters the body, then the first decision of Gorgias extends this analogy so as to include the soul. Now, the *pharmakon* is no more proportioned to the vegetal kingdom and the earth, but to the city. It would even be possible to argue that precisely the way Gorgias skips over the animals – this way is already an action of *logos* – indicates that the man of rhetoric is directly made into a political animal. As soon as he relates *pharmakon* and *logos*, Gorgias passes from the time of nature to the political time, where the performance of *pharmakon* starts to take on a new dimension which includes as its part the constitution of a *kosmos*. This ordering or arrangement, marked out by Derrida, would then be the first and most evident announcement of Plato's gesture. It is not by chance that in the dialogue called *Gorgias*, where the determination of *ti esti* and of *dunamis* of the rhetoric is being searched for,[33] the *kosmos* and the *taxis* become on the page 504a the key-words that will make it possible for Socrates to pass rather directly and continuously from the order of the human body's proportions (504a) to the order of the soul (504d), then through the order of each single thing (506d–e) to the order of city (507e1), and finally to the *kosmos* as a whole (*to holon*). If the name of *kosmos* as a whole is "order", it is thanks to the great power called "geometric equality" (*hé isotés hé geômetriké*, 508a6), the power that governs and binds together the four terms, that is: gods and men, heaven and earth (507e7–508a7). This bond of two relations, the analogical bond, is not just a simple enlargement of the first paragraph of *Encomion of Helen*. The *kosmos* of Gorgias and the *kosmos* Socrates speaks about in the *Gorgias* are and are not one and the same *kosmos*, because the heaven and earth of Socratic *kosmos* remind us of the fact that, in Plato's dialogues, the very name *kosmos* remains ambivalent as far as it can be used to design the order itself as well as what is ordered, that is the visible and corporeal world. Yet it is exactly this ambivalence that seems announced by the double use of the name *logos* by Gorgias (*Encomion* § 14).

To what Derrida says about this double use and the decision of analogy, we should add that contrary to the *logos* in the sense of relation, the *logos* in the sense of discourse or speech is determined by Gorgias as corporeal: the spoken word is the smallest and the most invisible of all bodies (*smikrotatôi sômati kai aphanestatôi*, § 8), the one that hides as a physical reserve beyond the divine actions of political persuasion. To introduce the *logismos* in the *logos* amounts, then, to subordinating the smallest bodies to the proportions which are not corporeal. This gesture, whose form makes it somehow akin to that of the *Timaeus*, where the reason succeeds to a certain degree in persuading the necessity, contains the germ of tension between the pre-Socratism and the Socrates of the dialogues, the tension born out of the double necessity to maintain the flow of *logos* and to stop it so that one could signify this or that determinate "something": the *ti* of *ti esti*.[34] The question *ti esti* asked by Socrates indicates a necessary separation of cosmology and philosophy, even if Gorgias seems to suggest that both of them could legitimately enter the realm of an omnipotent rhetoric and become its parts: *kosmos* is one of the possible but not fixed names of the world as a whole (*Timaeus* 28b3–5), but it is also a name of an analogical bond (*desmos*) of the four elements or simplest bodies that compose this whole (*Timaeus* 32c5–6). This double pre-Socratic use of the name *kosmos* – the proportion and what is proportioned – reproduces the limits of *ti esti*, the limits that Timaeus states very explicitly (50a5–c4), yet himself transgresses as soon as he starts to denote the whole of the corporeal *kosmos* by a demonstrative: as soon as he says "this *kosmos*" or "this whole".[35]

The double use of the name *logos* in paragraph 14 of the *Encomion of Helen* seems therefore to foreshadow the ambiguity of the name *kosmos* in the dialogues. Yet this more general feature should not let us forget that Plato revives the analogy of Gorgias almost literally, and that he does it at least twice. These two "refrains" are nevertheless very asymmetric to each other. In the *Theaetetus*, this analogy loses its resolution and then dispels, in the *Phaedrus*, it confirms itself and follows a new, already indicated direction: it makes possible to account for the *pharmakon* of writing.

As far as the *Theaetetus* is concerned, Socrates puts the analogy of *pharmakon* and *logos* in the mouth of Protagoras while picturing Protagoras' great apology.[36] However, in the version of Protagoras imagined by Socrates, the original analogy, strictly speaking, collapses: now, the *pharmaka* do not change the present state of body, but the patient's opinion about the states of his body, just as the education by means of *logos* reverses the disposition (*hexis*) of the soul. The drugs and the discourses, *pharmaka* and *logoi* (167a5), have just one and the same object, that is opinion as a truth of the sensation (*aisthésis*) that never ceases to change. The sensations and hence the opinions do change, but the degree of truth remains on each occasion the same. The analogy of Protagoras destroys the ground of the analogy of Gorgias, because there is no more *kosmos*, but only an universal flux. Immediately after he has compared the doctors and the Sophists (167a5), Protagoras, imagined by Socrates, compares the doctors and the farmers: in fact, the actions of the doctors are in the same relation to the bodies as those of the farmers are to the plants. The difference between the city and the nature ceases to be clear, because the plants themselves, just as the men, are endowed with sensations that are either malevolent or benevolent (167b6–c4). A short and ambiguous praise of a dialogical remedy or drug is then pronounced (167d2–168b2), but in this part of the text it is increasingly difficult to tell whether Protagoras (imagined by Socrates) addresses Socrates or whether, on the contrary, Socrates addresses Protagoras. Nothing remains but to admit that "everything moves" (168b4–5). Yet this *kineisthai ta panta* of Socrates–Protagoras reminds us that the universal flux does not us permit to concede (*sunchôrein*) expressions like "something" (*ti*) or "of something" (*tou*) or "mine" (*emou*) or "this" (*tode*) or "that" (*ekeino*) or any other name that would indicate a fixity or stability (157b2–5), and that according to nature, the *logos* could only say "becomes, is produced, perishes, changes". If everything always moves, there is no "something" (*ti*), and so nothing that would be in itself an agent (*to poioun*) or in itself a patient (*to paschon*) and, in the becoming, the producing agent may be called "such and such" but not "quality" (*to ... poioun poion ti all' ou poiotéta*, 182a8–9).[37] We understand that the *pharmakon* is neither active nor passive "in itself", but that its power manifests only where there is "something" active or passive. Such seems to be the condition of dialectics and also of writing, which becomes the theme of discourse when the analogy of Gorgias reappears in the *Phaedrus* (cf. 270b4-8).[38]

Even if the return and enlargement of the analogy of Gorgias in the *Phaedrus* (270b4-9) lead quickly to the question of writing, this passage is not entirely immediate. The analogy in question is evoked with respect to the resemblance of medicine and rhetoric, the first analyzing the nature of the body, the second the nature of the soul. Both of them have to rely on art (*techné*) and not on experience (*empeiria*), for only in such a way will medicine induce "by *pharmaka* and nurture" health to the body, while rhetoric will induce "by *logoi* and conduct conform to the laws" persuasion and virtue to the soul. It is, however, impossible to know the nature of the soul without knowing the nature of the whole (*tou holou phuseôs*, 270c2). And if we trust Hippocrates, adds Phaedrus, not even the body can be properly treated otherwise than through this method (270c3–4). Yet what is to be considered as the object of this remainder of Hippocrates? The whole composed of the soul and the body (that is, the nature of man), or simply the nature of the entire body as a part of the physical universe, as the *oude* in line 270c4 might well indicate? Without any decision concerning this ambiguity, Socrates admits that the discourse of Hippocrates is beautiful, but proposes at the same time to turn to the *logos* and to try to find whether it agrees with him (270c6–7). Socrates seems to distinguish between the *phusis* and the *logos*, and the reference to the Hippocratic inquiry *peri phuseôs* and to what *aléthés logos* says about it resembles a short and ironic version of the "second sailing" as depicted in the *Phaedo*. The explicit reference made formerly to Anaxagoras could confirm this point,[39] including the possible irony concerning the bond between politics and pre-Socratic philosophy. If this is really the case, then it is necessary that in the very heart of Socratic dialectics, the analogy of Gorgias be maintained and defended against any possible assimilation of the soul with the body, an assimilation to which Anaxagoras and Hippocrates seem to incline. In the knowledge of various species of souls resides both the force and the limit of rhetoric, while cosmology, and to a certain degree medicine,[40] are based on the hope that the mixed elements of the body will also allow for a persuasion. The dialectical rhetoric of Socrates understands the soul as a tissue of virtues, and consequently a mixture of activity and passivity. The good writing will strengthen precisely in this mixture and it will make it engender the equally good offspring. The good writing consists in the letters inscribed in the soul "according to the knowledge" (276a5–6). To all aspects of this inscription, Derrida pays so much attention as to the Egyptian story about Theuth and the invention of *grammata*. Moreover, the tissue of virtues and its governing by means of *logos* and according to the laws, does certainly remind us of some other passages analyzed in "Plato's Pharmacy", especially the text of the *Statesman* 310a1–5, which deals with the nuptial *pharmakon*, the divine bond created by art, tying together, into one single city, the naturally most dissembling parts of the virtue: the bond of which the political art of men seems to represent an analog.[41]

As Derrida reproduces and abundantly comments on the text of *Phaedrus* 276a1–277a4,[42] it is enough to underline its basic features and some of its details. The main character of this whole scene is is the so-called *allos logos*, another discourse, that is a discourse other than the *logos* both too silent and too talkative of the fixed writings which are incapable of any growth. This other *logos* is the brother of the first one, more exactly his legitimate brother. And because he was born, it is above all of his birth that one has to give an account (276a1–4). However, this is precisely what Socrates does not do, at least not strictly speaking, because he speaks exclusively about the germ and its transmission. Instead of directly explaining the generation of a living *logos*, Socrates offers its resuscitation by means of analogy. First, he proportions the *pharmakon* of writing, inscribed in the soul "according to the knowledge", to the grain of a plant sown in the earth; then he reduplicates the grain and it is only through this reduplication that the whole proportion with four terms comes to be: there is a *logos* similar to a weak seed, sown in the garden of Adonis, and another *logos*, similar to a strong seed sown in the patiently cultivated field.[43] In this return of the vegetal kingdom in the analogy of *logos* and *pharmakon*, the first alternative, that of writing and speech, steps aside to be replaced by the division of writing in two brothers. This reduplication of *logos* becomes even clearer a little bit later, where we learn that the well-sown *logos* continues to reproduce itself and becomes each time immortal: it no more needs the defense, because it will now itself defend us (276e6–277a4). The ultimate origin of the living *logos*, the origin of its seed or germ, remains hidden behind this becoming-immortal. The germ of the good writing never ceases to sprout each time and ever-more as a repetition of a precedent germ, as the immortal experience of *logoi* in us.[44] In this way, the origin or original production of *logos* comes to be replaced by the analogy which is at the same time new and inherited from a long pre-Socratic tradition.[45]

One can finally see what authorizes Derrida to affirm that "the conclusion of the *Phaedrus* is less a condemnation of writing in the name of present speech than a preference for one sort of writing over another, for the fertile trace over the sterile trace, for a seed that engenders because it is planted inside over a seed scattered wastefully outside: at the risk of *dissemination*".[46] The analogy that comprehends this risk is an analogy in the strict sense of the word. It is the relation or *logos* of two different relations:

> the relation of simulacrum-writing to what it represents – the true writing (the real writing because it is real, authentic, corresponding to its value, conform to its essence, writing in the soul of him who possesses the *epistémé*) – this relation is *analogous* to the relation of strong, fertile seeds engendering necessary, lasting, nourishing produce (fructiferous seeds) to weak, easily exhausted, superfluous seeds giving rise to ephemeral produce (floriferous seeds).[47]

This summary invites us to consider a cryptogamy of philosophical writing where life and death are at stake: not just the survival of an individual, but the survival of a philosophy which, at the end of the *Phaedrus*, seems to inscribe in the great Greek preoccupation with the transmission of immortal glory, *kleos aphthiton*, the glory that the poet weaves into his song "as the resonant and imperishable fame of the hero".[48] For the most important moment of this passage consists in the reappearance of the theme of immortality in the shape of *sperma athanaton*. Yet this new immortality is completely different from the immortality of soul as depicted in Socrates' palinode, because the writing in the soul seems to replace both its immortality and its direct contact with the "hyperouranian" beings. The *Phaedrus* seems to contain in both its living and written body an analog of the two "series of immortality" indicated by the oracle of Diotima in the *Symposium*:[49] engendering according to the body and according to the soul (206b7). The first one incarnates in the engendering of human beings which has no beginning and no end; the second one presupposes the passage through the soul's contact with the beautiful that Diotima places "high up" and that has no body.

The texts of the *Phaedrus* and the *Symposium* are certainly very different, yet as far as the question of analogy is concerned, they do share one common feature: the impossibility of conciliating the two immortalities (hence the four terms) within one single schema of *logos*, within one single analogy that would not overlap with a genealogy which (if it ties together the humans and not men and gods) represents a difference of degree but not of nature. In fact, we find here the same feature that characterizes the analogy of good and sun in book VI of the *Republic*,[50] where the constitutive and irresolvable tension of analogy and genealogy originates in the same movement of *logos* expressed by Socrates, whether Socrates claims to be its father or not. Yet Socrates resembles rather an intermediate being, and this still by virtue of analogy, picked up by Derrida, of Socratic and Sophistic *pharmakon*. This intermediary is no other than that *erôs* of the *Symposium*, son of Poros and Penia, a double being whose nature is neither immortal nor mortal, who in one and the same day sometimes flourishes and sometimes dies, and spends the time of his life philosophizing, being a "fearsome sorcerer (*deinos goés*), magician (*pharmakeus*), Sophist (*sophistés*)".[51] If, in the *Phaedrus* and the *Symposium*, there is an undecided space where the differences of degree and the analogies overlap, this space may well be the space of what Derrida calls "pharmacy". The *pharmakon* is also a prescription of analogy, for instance of this analogy which, in the *Phaedrus*, is being elaborated in the wake of Hippocrates and Gorgias.

In Plato, such an elaboration seems to play the role of an indication or a trace of the very life of *logos*. It remains to add that this trace, both irreducible and ambiguous (cf. *Cratylus* 408c2-d4), could serve as a starting point of another and more complete inquiry into analogy in Derrida's texts on Plato. Derrida himself invites us to do so: in other passages of "Plato's Pharmacy", the question of the life of *logos* and its kinship leads from the *pharmakon* of writing to the analogy of good and sun in the *Republic*, and this movement is guided by several partially-quoted and partially-constructed analogies.[52] And if these constructions prevent the sense of the text from becoming univocal, it is still by virtue of a Platonic analogy of being and quality of discourse about that being. In the apparatus of this pharmacy, there may be two articulations which are critical in the strict sense of the word, namely two inscriptions of the *Timaeus* in the Socratic *logos* of the *pharmakon*.[53]

But it is only with *Khôra* that we shall have to return to these articulations in order to question the conditions and the limits of analogy as such. The short present commentary tried only to emphasize that, with the exception of *Glas*, "Plato's Pharmacy" was perhaps, and for a good reason, the text of Derrida most abounding in analogies. It is precisely why, in this text, the simple return to Plato gives way to the return of Plato, author of written dialogues.

Charles University, Prague

Notes

¹ "Plato's Pharmacy", p. 159/"La pharmacie de Platon", p. 183. "Plato's Pharmacy" will be quoted (sometimes modified) from Barbara Johnson's translation from *Dissemination*, University of Chicago Press, 1981, pp. 61–171. The second page number refers to the French edition of 1972, *La Dissémination*, Paris, Seuil, pp. 69–197. The transliteration of Greek respects the differences between "La pharmacie de Platon" and the second edition of *Khôra*, Paris, Galilée, 1993.
² Cf. "Lettre à un ami japonais", *Psyché. Inventions de l'autre*, Paris, Galilée, 1987, p. 392.
³ *Positions*, Paris, Minuit, 1972, p. 58.
⁴ These marks are never the occasion of "une solution dans la forme de la dialectique spéculative" (ibid.). This passage is partially quoted in C. G. Lazos, "Les deux répétitions ou le coup double du *pharmakon*", *Revue de philosophie ancienne*, VII, 1, 1989, p. 102. The last part of the sentence consists in a series of "indecidables" where the *pharmakon* comes first.
⁵ Cf. Aristotle, *Parts of Animals* I, 4, 643b16–19 and 5, 645b6–10. This second passage indicates to the readers of Derrida that the *pharmakon* which flows in a text defined as a living being (*zôion*) is not necessarily one and the same nor even similar in every text. Which is precisely the case in Plato's dialogues.
⁶ Cf. *Politiques de l'amitié*, Paris, Galilée, 1984, pp. 86–88 on the "classical concept of decision". This is equally one of the subjects of *Force de loi*, Paris, Galilée, 1994.
⁷ "Economimesis", *Mimesis des articulations*, Paris, Galilée, 1975, p. 74. Cf. *La voix et le phénomène*, Paris, PUF, 1967, p. 13; *L'archéologie du frivole*, Paris, Galilée, 1973, pp. 51–70, 81, 84; *La vérité en peinture*, Paris, Flammarion, 1978, pp. 43, 88. See equally "Force et signification",*L'écriture et la différence*, Paris, Seuil, 1967, pp. 31–32, and "Violence et métaphysique", ibid., pp 147–148, 211. Some of these passages are commented upon in R. Gasché, *The Tain of the Mirror. Derrida and the Philosophy of Reflection*, Harvard University Press, 1986, pp. 302–307.
⁸ Cf. E. Przywara, *Analogia entis*, Josef Kösel & Friedrich Pustet, München, 1932, pp. 68–69, 100–101. One thinks immediately of analogy of the *Republic* VI–VII, of the relation between the good and the sun.
⁹ In *Khôra*, Derrida underscores this moment in order to proportion the birth of the *kosmos* and the origin of the Athenians. For *khôra* of the *Timaeus*, the civic *khôra* and the reading of Derrida, see N. Loraux, "Le retour de l'exclu", *Le passage des frontières. Autour du travail de Jacques Derrida*, Colloque de Cerisy, Galilée, Paris, 1994, pp. 151–159.
¹⁰ Cf. *Phaedo* 96a1–102a1.
¹¹ See, precisely in the *Phaedo*, the final description of the "true earth" of which "our" earth is but a pitiful analogy that, moreover, reminds us of the cavern of the *Republic*; see equally *Philebus* 27c3–31b1, *Gorgias* 504a–508a.
¹² For this process, see three texts by P. Aubenque: "Ambiguïté ou analogie de l'être?", *Le langage. Actes du XIII. Congrès des Sociétés de philosophie de langue française*

– *Genève 1966*, La Baconnière, Neuchatel, pp. 12–13; "Les origines de la doctrine de l'analogie de l'être. Sur l'histoire d'un contresens", *Les Etudes philosophiques*, 1978, pp. 3–12; "Zur Entstehung der pseudo–aristotelischen Lehre von der Analogie des Seins", *Aristoteles. Werk und Wirkung*, Zweiter Band, hrsg. von J. Wiesner, De Gruyter, Berlin &New York, 1987, pp. 233–248.

[13] Cf. *Sauf le nom*, Paris, Galilée, 1993, pp. 72–75.
[14] "Plato's Pharmacy", p. 166/ "La pharmacie de Platon", p. 193.
[15] The analogy is conditionned by the *poiésis*. See Aristotle, *Poetics* 1457b16–34. For a commentary on this passage, see "La mythologie blanche. La métaphore dans le texte philosophique", *Marges de la philosophie*, Minuit, Paris, 1972, pp. 275–276, and above all pp. 288–290 with a parenthesis concerning the *Republic* VI–VII.
[16] "Plato's Pharmacy", p. 128/"La pharmacie de Platon", p. 146. It is still through a decision of analogy that this pharmacy is being explicitly proportioned to Rousseau and Saussure (cf. "Plato's Pharmacy", p. 96, n. 43 /"La pharmacie de Platon", p. 109, n. 40; pp. 159/159/182–183) and also, perhaps chiefly, to Kant's *Critique of the Pure Reason* (see page 126/144, one of the most enigmatical of the whole text). Some other analogies are only indicated: one may reread for instance page 152/175 of the "Pharmacy" and the beginning of "Le puits et la pyramide" (*Marges de la philosophie*, Minuit, Paris, 1972, p. 81), which would make us realize how the *pharmacy* proportions to Hegel's theory of sign without changing the explicit meaning of one single word of Plato.
[17] Temporarily, because they will serve to mark the transcription of oral as well as the textual quotations. The invention of inverted commas seems to go back to the French edition of Ramus' *Dialectics* (1555). The parts of the texts marked in this way are at the same time the translations (cf. A. Compagnon, *La seconde main ou le travail de la citation*, Paris, Seuil, 1979, pp. 246–247). According to Derrida, there could be a common root of the internal differentiation of a language and the origin of the plurality of languages ("Plato's Pharmacy", p. 88/100).
[18] Cf. *Philebus* 18b6–d3; *Theaetetus* 203a1–e5; *Sophist* 253a4–6.
[19] Cf. *Meno* 81b4–d6.
[20] "Plato's Pharmacy", p. 115/"La pharmacie de Platon", p. 131.
[21] Ibid., p. 116/132.
[22] *Encomium of Helen* (DK 82 B 11), § 2. The most recent edition is due to Francesco Donadi, *Encomoi di Elena*, Bolletino dell'Instituto di Filologia Greca, supplemento 7, Universita di Padova, "L'Erma" di Bretschneider, Roma, 1982. A new French translation, with some emendations of the text, was published in Barbara Cassin, *L'effet sophistique*, Paris, Gallimard, 1995, pp. 141–148.
[23] "Plato's Pharmacy", p. 115/"La pharmacie de Platon", p. 131.
[24] *Encomium of Helen*, §1.
[25] "Plato's Pharmacy", p. 116/"La pharmacie de Platon", p. 133.
[26] Cf. *Theaetetus* 186a10–b1, where Theaetetus wants to "proportion" the three dimensions of time.
[27] Cf. *Encomion of Helen*, §§ 10–11.
[28] *On the Places in man* (*Peri topôn tôn kata anthrôpon*), 45, 1 (ed. R. Joly, Paris, CUP, 1978).
[29] *On the Nature of Man* (*Peri phusios anthrôpou*) 6, 3 (ed., translated into French and commented by J. Jouanna, *Corpus medicorum grecorum* I, 1,3, Berlin, Akademie-Verlag, 1975; I quote the modified translation of W. H. S. Jones, *Hippocrates* IV, Loeb Classical Library, 1931). It is important to underline that the action of *pharmakon* does not limit itself to the evacuation of the humour most akin to itself.
[30] "Plato's Pharmacy", p. 117/"La pharmacie de Platon", p. 133.
[31] Ibid., pp. 119/135–136.
[32] Ibid., p. 119/136.

³³ *Gorgias* 447c1–d1.
³⁴ Cf. *Theaetetus* 157b2–5.
³⁵ Cf. *Timaeus* 29a3 *hode ho kosmos*; 29b1 *tode to kosmos*; and 29d6–e1 *to pan tode*. This way of speech is an old one and may have been related to the constitution of the world from four elements (cf. Hippocrates, *On the nature of man* 7, 50, with a probable reference to Diogenes of Apollonia, DK 64b2). From the point of view of Timaeus, discussed by Derrida in *Khôra*, the corporeal *kosmos* or *ouranos* should not be called *tode* ou *touto*, but only *toiouton*, "such as". Timaeus, rather surprisingly, uses this pronoun while speaking about the intelligible model which he denotes on the page 28a as *toiouton ti paradeigma*. Even if the context is irreducibly different, one may be reminded of Socrates' palinody in the *Phaedrus*, where everything divine is said to be *kalon, sophon, agathon kai pan ho ti toiouton* (246e1).
³⁶ *Theaetetus* 167a2 sq. In "Plato's Pharmacy", Derrida quotes this passage in a long footnote (p. 150–151, n. 71/p. 173–174, n. 66). This footnote is parallel to a quotation of the *Phaedrus* 267a–c (the gardens of Adonis) and follows very closely two paragraphs concerning the analogy of writing and agriculture.
³⁷ For the textual intricacies of these lines, see the note of Michel Narcy in his French translation of *Theaetetus*: *Théétète*, Paris, GF-Flammarion, 1994, pp. 351–352, n. 312. The substantive "quality", *poiotés*, does not appear in any other of Plato's dialogues nor in any known pre-Socratic text.
³⁸ For the sake of brevity, we may only indicate the similarity between the "critique of language" in the *Theaetetus* and in the *Timaeus* 49b–50a. In the *Cratylus*, the syntagm "everything moves" receives the form *panta khôrei kai ouden menei* (402a8–9), partially identical with the expression *khôrei de panta* from the Hippocratic treatise *On the regimen* (*Peri diaités* I, 5). For a possible comparison with *khôra*, cf. S. Benardete, "Physics and Tragedy: On Plato's *Cratylus*", *Ancient Philosophy* I, 2, 1981, p. 135.
³⁹ The expression *adoleschia kai meteorologia peri phuseôs* (270a1) does not look like a compliment. It could, however, refer once again to the *Encomium of Helen*, § 13.
⁴⁰ Cf. *On the Places in man*, 46, 1–3.
⁴¹ "Plato's Pharmacy", p. 126/"La pharmacie de Platon", p. 144. It is this *pharmakon* of dissemblance and of what is heterogeneous that Derrida proportions to the transcendental imagination. One is tempted to speak about an analogy of analogy. The page 126/144, complex and enigmatical, calls for a separate analysis in another text.
⁴² "Plato's Pharmacy", p. 148–155/ "La pharmacie de Platon", pp. 171–179. On the gardens of Adonis, see also M. Detienne, *Les jardins d'Adonis. Mythologies des aromates en Grèce*, Paris, Gallimard, 1972.
⁴³ "Plato's Pharmacy" offers a more exact and complete formulation of this analogy on the page 150/173.
⁴⁴ Cf. *Philebus* 15d7–8.
⁴⁵ If, according to Derrida, the *pharmakon* of the *Phaedrus* functions in his reading of Plato in a way analogous to his reading of Rousseau's supplement ("Plato's Pharmacy", p. 96, n. 43/ "La pharmacie de Platon", p. 109, n. 40), we must conclude that the science that writes itself and sprouts in the soul is proportional to the birth of a human society: "the post-original degradation is analogous to the pre-original repetition" (*De la grammatologie*, Paris, Minuit, 1967, p. 377).
⁴⁶ "Plato's Pharmacy", p. 149/ "La pharmacie de Platon", p. 172.
⁴⁷ Ibid., p. 150/173.
⁴⁸ J. Svenbro, *Phrasikleia. Anthropologie de la lecture en Grèce ancienne*, Paris, La Découverte, 1988, p. 76. For *kleos*, see also G. Nagy, *The Best of the Achaeans: Concept of the Hero in Archaic Greek Poetry*, Johns Hopkins University Press, Baltimore, 1979, and "Another Look at *KLEOS APHTHITON*", *Würzburger Jahrbücher für die Altertumswissenschaft* 7, 1981, pp. 113–116.

[49] Cf. *Symposium* 208c–209e, and also *Laws* IV, 721b–c (immortality of the human race). J. Svenbro compares these two texts not only to the formula *kleos aphthiton*, but also to the expression *sperma aphthiton*, "imperishable seed", used by Pindar in *Pythian* IV, 42 sq. Cf. Svenbro, op. cit., pp. 76–78. I can only point out that Svenbro shows very well that the "writing in the soul" is not just Plato's invention, but rather the appropriation of a *topos* of lyric and tragic poetry (cf. pp. 178–206).

[50] Cf. L. Couloubaritsis, "Le caractère mythique de l'analogie du Bien dans *République* VI", *Diotima* 12, 1984, pp. 71–80. Cf. also the discussion between J. Barnes ("Le soleil de Platon vu avec des lunettes analytiques") and M. Dixsaut ("L'analogie intenable"), *Rue Descartes* nos 1–2, 1991, pp. 81–92, 93–120.

[51] *Symposium* 203d7; "Plato's Pharmacy", p. 117/"La pharmacie de Platon", p. 134.

[52] "Plato's Pharmacy", pp. 75–84/"La pharmacie de Platon", pp. 84–95.

[53] Cf. ibid., pp. 100–101/114–115 (*Timaeus* 89a–d), and 160–161/185–187 (*Timaeus* 48e–51e, 52b–c).

Chapter 4

Daydream

John Sallis

– der Traum ist ausgeträumt.
(E. Husserl)

It is imperative.
It is even the imperative of imperatives.
One is to begin – so says this imperative – by turning to the things themselves.

This is what is required in order that thinking be rigorous: that it proceed from things themselves, that it take its bearings solely from them, that it take entirely from them the truth that would be declared, itself contributing nothing except the detaching of that truth from the things themselves, its detachment in a form that can be declared, its transcription. It would be difficult to say what belongs to – and what delimits – philosophy that does not also lie within the arc of this turn. Or at the points from which and to which the arc swings. Or rather, in the intervals that open at these points, displacing them, erasing them. Once one has caught a glimpse of these openings, one can declare – reproducing, almost, the very opening in question – that the detachment of truth from the things themselves is not itself taken from the things themselves, that transcription cannot but transmute εἰς ἄλλο γένος. And turning back toward the beginning, one can declare also that the very turn to the things themselves opens an interval, a moment of near-blindness, an indeterminate space across which one's vision would first come to adhere to the things themselves – at least to the extent that, between this and the other interval, rigor is not merely a dream that one would finally have dreamed out. But this interval, that of the beginning and of the deferral of beginning, this interval in which, as Timaeus says, "we intend to make a suitable beginning [... μέλλομεν ἄρξεσθαι κατὰ τρόπον]" (*Tim.* 54a), the duplicity of the word (μέλλω) opening precisely this interval (to intend to begin, to be about to begin, is also to delay, to defer the very beginning that one is about to make) – this interval would surely be difficult to distinguish from a dream. Difficult – that is, χαλεπόν, hence also: troublesome, even dangerous.

This indicator, the word χαλεπόν, is one of the most decisive in the *Timaeus*, and its resonance ought not be lost as one turns back to the dream, returning to it, as near the end of a text by Jacques Derrida that bears – even in French – the English title "Tense": "Return to the dream, then, the dream that we never abandoned, for still 'we are imagining that we are dreaming.' We recall that Plato says of χώρα that we perceive it as in a dream (*Timaeus* 52b–c)."[1] The self-citation refers to the opening words of "Tense": "Let us imagine. Let us imagine that we are dreaming."[2] Dreaming of what? Dreaming, in French, of inventing an *autre temps*. Derrida asks that the translator leave these two last words in their original language, and he leaves this request itself, set in parentheses, in the text of "Tense". This *autre temps* is to be a gift, invented and offered in the time of the dream. Unless – says Derrida – the recipient has already invented it himself: "Unless – and we are now in the time of the dream – unless he has already done it himself."[3] In this case the economy of the gift would be interrupted or at least put in question: for how could one give time to someone who, through his own invention, already had time? And how could the recipient give something in turn, something of comparable value, which could only be, again, to give time? How – except by differentiation? And by insistence. By insisting that it be, always and even at the same time (*tout à la fois*, ἅμα), an *autre temps*.

A time as other, as marked by alterity. Such time as that of the dream of the χώρα. Or rather, what one would call such, were it not in every respect anterior to the operation of such structures as that of the *such*.

Let us begin by taking this time as that of the χώρα, as the time of which one would also dream in dreaming of the χώρα. Then it would be indeed an *autre temps*, a time other than time, a time before time, a time "before everything", as Derrida says, "the absolute antecedent".[4] It would be a time different even from the time of day, the time measured out by the course of the sun across the sky. Heidegger takes the day to be indeed "the 'most natural' measure of time."[5] But the time of the χώρα, this *autre temps*, is not measured by the day and by the course of the sun. It is a time anterior to such measure, a time anterior – it would seem – to all measure. There is (*il y a*) this unmeasured, measureless time before the sun comes to bring measure and illumination to all things. There is (*il y a*) this time before the day, before sunrise – a time that is not just night, not just the time after nightfall with its promise of the coming sunrise, but rather an *autre nuit*, "*l'autre nuit [qui] est toujours autre*".[6] A night that never becomes day, ever-prevailing darkness. Like Hades.

The time of the χώρα is not yet even a time of imagination. It is not a time in which one could imagine; one could not even imagine imagining in this time. Not, at least, if imagining is taken to consist in somehow bringing images to presence before, as we say, the mind's eye. For the time to which Timaeus' discourse on the χώρα is directed is a time before the generation of the heaven (πρὸ τῆς γενέσεως [*Tim.* 48b; cf. 52d]). It is a time in which there are not yet any images whatsoever, a time when – in the absence of the artisan god (53b), while he is, as it were, idle – even the simplest of things (of what will be transmuted into sensible images), fire, air, water, and earth, are *not yet themselves*, are not yet properly images but only *traces* of themselves as such (ἴχνη ... ἔχοντα αὐτῶν ἄττα [53b]). And yet, one can dream of the χώρα as it was in this time; perhaps even one *must* have such a dream if anything binding is to be said of the χώρα. Indeed it will turn out that the force of the dream lies in its power to bring forth an image of the χώρα, of the χώρα as it was in the time before there were images. In the time of the dream there will be brought forth an image of the χώρα in an *autre temps* when there were not yet any images at all, or rather, as it would have been in that *autre temps*, had it been such that one could say simply that it had been, had it been such that one could then have said of it simply: it *is*.

But when it comes to the dream of the time of the χώρα, perhaps nothing can be said *simply*, perhaps nothing can *simply* be said. Derrida has, above all, called attention to the precautions that any such discourse will now have to observe, on pain of violating in its very form, in the rhetorical resources that it puts in play, the configuration determining that which, in this regard, is to be said:

> Almost all the interpreters of the *Timaeus* gamble here [*misent à cet endroit*] on the resources of rhetoric without asking about them. They speak tranquilly about metaphors, images, similes. They pose no questions about this tradition of rhetoric, which places at their disposal a reserve of concepts that are very useful but that are built upon this distinction between the sensible and the intelligible, which is precisely that to which the thought of the χώρα can no longer be accommodated.[7]

One will not be entitled, then, to take the resources of classical rhetoric for granted, to let discourse now on the χώρα be filled out with concepts such as that of metaphor, of simile, and of image. The same will need to be said even of concept, of the "concept" of concept, which likewise is built on the distinction between the sensible and the intelligible, the very distinction that the *Timaeus* puts into question precisely at the moment when it comes to speak of the χώρα. On the other hand, not taking any of these classical determinations for granted does not amount simply to prohibiting them from entering a discourse now on the χώρα. But if they are to be put in play – as I have proposed putting *image* into play – their sense must in every case be determined strictly from the Platonic text itself. Even if, as in the case of *image*, this very text, the *Timaeus*, also puts this determination in question.

If in this connection one were to insist on retaining a discourse of imagination, the demands would be still more difficult. An *autre temps* in which one could not even imagine imagining: that which is in this *autre temps* – though without itself quite *being*, without quite being itself – is then in the dream to be brought forth (allowed to arrive) in the guise of an image. What must be proper to imagination (and how abysmally must it be expropriated) in order that it let arrive images of that in relation to which one cannot even imagine imagining? One suspects that this propriety would turn out to be no less strange than that alluded to in the title (and text) of a short prose piece by Beckett: "Imagination Dead Imagine."[8]

Before taking up the return to the dream as Derrida has marked it in "Tense," let me underline again the strangeness of that which – without quite being – belongs to the *autre temps*. Not that the χώρα is not also in the time after the god has fabricated both the cosmos and this time itself: yet even as it perdures in leaving its marks on the fabricated cosmos, it remains *autre*, it "*est toujours autre*". Its alterity comes to be most pointedly in question when one considers the bearing of the χώρα with respect to being. Derrida introduces such considerations explicitly in *Khôra*:

> But if Timaeus names it receptacle (*dekhomenon*) or place [*lieu*] (*khôra*), these names do not designate an essence, the stable being of an *eidos*, since *khôra* is neither of the order of the *eidos* nor of the order of mimemes, of the images of the *eidos*, which come to imprint themselves on it – which thus is *not* and does not belong to the two known or recognized genera of being.[9]

It should not go unnoticed that in this passage a kind of translation of the word χώρα has insinuated itself, a translation that has indeed a venerable history, going back at least to Calcidius' Latin translation of the *Timaeus* in the fifth century AD, in which χώρα is rendered as *locus*. Still, *locus* and *lieu* are translations[10] and cannot but raise interminable questions when it is a matter, as with the word χώρα (assuming it to be a word), of a word that threatens the very possibility of translation, that threatens to disrupt that detour through a common signified that has nearly always been taken to constitute translation.

Yet the focal issue in the passage – the issue I want to underline – is that of the bearing of the χώρα with respect to being. Within the discursive rhythm of the *Timaeus* the χώρα is counted – repeatedly – along with other kinds (γένη) that could be counted as kinds of being. One would say, then, of the χώρα that it is a third kind of being, counted after the first kind (intelligible) and the second kind (sensible). And yet, the designation cannot stand: for only the first kind (the intelligible εἴδη) can be called *being*, whereas the second kind is generation (γένεσις, τὸ γιγνόμενον) and the third kind is the *in which* (τὸ ἐν ᾧ) or the receptacle (ὑποδοχή) of all generation. If the second kind can be said to have some slight share in being, so that a sensible thing can be called *a being*, there would seem to be little or no possibility of extending such a name to the third kind. It is neither being nor a being, neither an intelligible being nor a sensible being; as Derrida says, it "does not belong to the two known or recognized genera of being". If it is a being in any sense whatsoever, then it would have to be so in a sense of being beyond being, in a sense of being in excess of being. Even if, short of venturing to think such excess, one were to say that it is nothing, an immediate qualification, a kind of retraction, would be required, as in a recent text where Derrida writes: "Khôra is nothing (nothing of being or of present), but not the Nothing that, in Dasein's anxiety, would open again to the question of being."[11] From being it is even more remote, more alien, than every nothing that still, however obliquely, opens onto being. The χώρα remains other, *elle est toujours autre*.

In "Tense" Derrida recalls the phrase with which being in excess of being is most forcefully expressed in the Platonic text, a phrase that has been taken up and made to play an important role by Heidegger and Levinas, the phrase that Plato reserves for what (in the interest of economy) can be translated as *the good*: the phrase is ἐπέκεινα τῆς οὐσίας, *beyond being*. Recalling this phrase, Derrida asks about its pertinence as regards the χώρα, that is, whether the phrase is suitable for saying the relevant excess. He asks, in particular, why it happens that Plato does not use the phrase in this way: "And yet why does not Plato say that χώρα is ἐπέκεινα τῆς οὐσίας? Why is that so difficult to say and to think?"[12] Elsewhere, even more forcefully, no longer in the form of a question, he writes: "Khôra ... does not even announce itself as 'beyond being' ['*au-delà de l'être*']."[13]

It is as if there were a double excess, or rather, not *a* double but two excesses, two ways of being beyond being, two ways that would be themselves unrelated, uncrossed, without even a moment of coincidence sufficient to allow the phrase ἐπέκεινα τῆς οὐσίας to be extended from one to the other. In posing the question of this double excess in which each would also seem absolutely to exceed the other, Derrida has opened an immense domain of questions; and they are questions of the utmost pertinence for the effort today to think the limit of metaphysics, to think being at the limit of metaphysics.

In this regard I will restrict myself to a single point, to a mere indication of one point – among many, no doubt – from which one might develop certain of the questions belonging to this domain opened up by Derrida's texts on the *Timaeus*. But even before marking that point, let me call attention to the passage in Book 6 of the *Republic* in which Socrates speaks of the good in its peculiar excess. It is a matter of declaring, first of all, that the to-be and being (τὸ εἶναί τε καὶ τὴν οὐσίαν) belong to things on account of the good; and then that "the good is not being but is still beyond being [ἐπέκεινα τῆς οὐσίας], exceeding it [ὑπερέχοντος] in dignity and power" (*Rep.* 509b). One presumes that the power (δύναμις) of the good by which it exceeds being lies in its being empowered to bestow being upon whatever is, to bring being to belong to things. But its excess is not only one of power but also of dignity. Without venturing to suppose what might constitute the dignity of the good in this ontological connection, what dignity could conceivably signify here, let me merely note that πρεσβεία, which one readily translates as *dignity*, also means *age* or *seniority*. The verb πρεσβεύω can mean, among other things: to take the place of others by right of seniority, to rule over others by virtue of being the oldest. The good is older than being, and it rules over all beings by first bestowing upon them their being. The good is anterior to being and beings; it belongs to a time before being and beings, an *autre temps*.

In any case one should not overlook the very remarkable response that Glaucon offers to Socrates' declaration about the excessiveness of the good: "And Glaucon, quite ridiculously, said, 'Apollo, what a demonic excess'" (*Rep.* 509c).

What, then, about the relation – or even nonrelation – between the excess of the good and that of the χώρα? As Derrida notes, Plato's text makes no direct reference to such a relation; or, more precisely, it never extends to the χώρα the designation ἐπέκεινα τῆς οὐσίας. And yet, there is a point – and this is the one I want to mark – where the good and the χώρα are brought into a very remarkable proximity. This point comes in the passage at the beginning of Book 7 of the *Republic* where Socrates speaks of "our nature in its education and lack of education" by asking Glaucon to imagine an underground cave-like dwelling and its inhabitants who, though initially bound, come to be released and to ascend into the openness and the light above. Toward the end of the passage, Socrates speaks of what sounds like a culmination of the ascent: from looking at reflections of things in water, the liberated prisoner could come to look at things themselves and then could turn his gaze upward so as to behold things in the heaven and the heaven itself, more easily at night, looking at the light of the stars and the moon. Socrates concludes: "Then finally I suppose he would be able to look upon the sun – not its appearances [its phantoms – φαντάσματα] in water or in some other base [ἕδρα], but the sun itself by itself in its own χώρα – and behold how it is" (*Rep.* 516b).

In the commentary that Socrates conjoins to the entire passage, he correlates the various sites and stages with those already delimited in Book 6 with respect to the affections in the soul and the corresponding levels of disclosure of beings.[14] On the basis of this correlation, together with the earlier parallel by which the sun is said to be "an offspring the good begot in proportion [ἀνάλογον] with itself" (*Rep.* 508b–c), one can carry over what is said of the sun into something to be said of the good. Here it is not a matter of drawing uncritically on the traditional rhetorical concept of metaphor but of recognizing that this is one of those points in the

Platonic texts – perhaps even the single most decisive one – where the very sense of metaphor comes to be established, where the very domains are first conjoined between which metaphors will, from that point on, transport sense into sense: "as the good is in the intelligible region [ἐν τῷ νοητῷ τόπῳ] with respect to intelligence [νοῦς] and what is intellected, so the sun is in the visible region with respect to sight and what is seen" (*Rep.* 508c).

What, then, of the χώρα and of the proximity of its excess to that of the good? The connection is clear enough in the case of the good's offspring. In this case the proximity is linked to the propriety of the sun: it is precisely when one no longer sees its phantoms, precisely when one looks at it itself by itself (αὐτὸν καθ' αὑτον), when one sees the sun proper – it is precisely then that one sees it in its χώρα. Thus, to see it in its χώρα is not at all to see it in relation to something else rather than as itself and by itself; on the contrary, seeing it as itself by itself *is* precisely seeing it in its χώρα. Only in its χώρα does the sun come to be beheld properly, as itself and by itself.

Especially in those passages where attention turns to the apparent culmination of the ascent, Socrates almost invariably inserts disclaimers, reservations, references to opinion and to how things seem, all of which serve to divert or defer the movement he is describing or feigning to describe.[15] For example, in the midst of describing the ascent to the intelligible region, he abruptly inserts the following remarks before then going on to speak of the good: "A god doubtless knows if it chances to be true. At all events this is how the appearance appears to me" (*Rep.* 517b). But even apart from such strategies, questions cannot but accumulate around what Socrates says of the sun in its χώρα. Not the least among them is the question of blindness: for one could look upon the sun itself by itself, beholding it in its χώρα, only at the risk of blindness. In another celebrated passage Socrates cites this risk as precisely what provoked his turn from things to λόγοι, his δεύτερος πλοῦς (Phaedo 99d–e). Does the χώρα also pose such a risk, at least in its proximity to the sun proper? Is there, then, provocation to turn from vision to λόγος? Furthermore, what about the metaphorical move, the translating of the vision of the sun over into the intellection or hyperintellection of the good? What happens to the χώρα in this translation? Can the χώρα be carried over from the sensible to the intelligible, even though, as the *Timaeus* demonstrates, it is neither sensible nor intelligible? Can there be, then, a metaphorizing of the χώρα? If not, then how is one to read the passage on the χώρα of the sun, that is, how is one to read it within the metaphorics explicitly established in this very context? How – through what kind of translation – is the χώρα of the sun to be carried over into the χώρα of the good? Is there a χώρα of the good? And is the good to be looked upon itself by itself precisely when it is beheld in its χώρα? What is required in order to behold the good in its χώρα? How is the χώρα itself – if there be a χώρα itself – to be beheld?

How is the χώρα to be apprehended? How is it to be perceived, assuming that some sense of perception is pertinent to its apprehension.

In a dream. The χώρα is to be apprehended in a dream.

Or as in a dream. This precisely is what Derrida says, what he ascribes to Plato, though one will want to add that what is said in this regard comes in the voice of Timaeus.

In a dream. Or as in a dream. What is the difference marked by the *as*? Does it express only some vague similarity between the state of dreaming and that in which one would apprehend the χώρα? Or is the dream integral to such apprehension so that the *as* would mark only a certain distancing, a hermeneutic interval? Derrida observes, in any case, that this apprehension, linked somehow to a dream, is thereby exposed to two contrary effects: it "could just as well deprive it of lucidity as confer upon it a power of divination."[16]

Here it must suffice merely to indicate these two contrary moments.

The reference to the dream comes in a passage at the center of the *Timaeus*, the passage in which this third kind finally comes to be called χώρα. This passage (*Tim.* 52a–d) I call the chorology. Timaeus tells exactly how the χώρα is to be apprehended: it is "to be apprehended, with nonsensation [μετ' ἀναισθησίας], by a sort of bastard reckoning [λογισμῷ τινὶ νόθῳ]" (*Tim.* 52b). Thus, it is not to be apprehended by perception, if the sense of perception is determined by the traditional connection to αἴσθησις, that is, if it is taken as sense-perception. Yet this does not entail that the apprehension of the χώρα is a matter of intellectual or noetic vision (νόησις). On the contrary, just as the introduction of the χώρα puts in question the very opposition between αἰσθητόν and νοητόν, so likewise its apprehension is not such as can be confined to this opposition and its field.

It is just at the point where the apprehension is called "bastard reckoning", something "hardly trustworthy", that Timaeus refers to the dream of the χώρα: "And looking toward which we dream [of it] and affirm that it is necessary that all that is be somewhere in some place [τόπος] and occupy [or: hold back – κατέχον] some χώρα; and that that which is neither on earth nor anywhere in the heavens is nothing" (*Tim.* 52b).

In the dream the χώρα is pictured as the place in which all that is must be. In the oneiric vision the χώρα – or rather, its dream-image – hovers before us as a place so all-encompassing that whatever is set apart from it can only be nothing. But what is there in a dream? Socrates tells Glaucon what there is in a dream, tells him through a series of questions posed in a passage in Book 5 of the *Republic*:

> Is the man who holds that there are beautiful things but does not hold that there is beauty itself and who, if someone leads him to the knowledge of it, is not able to follow – is he, in your opinion, living in a dream or is he awake? Consider it. Does dreaming, whether one is asleep or awake, not consist in believing a likeness of something to be not a likeness but rather the thing itself to which it is like? (*Rep.* 476c)

Glaucon agrees that such a man is dreaming, and Socrates then goes on to contrast the dreamer with a man who believes that there is a beautiful itself and who is able to distinguish between it and its images, the many beautiful things. Glaucon agrees that the latter man is quite awake. Formalizing, one could say: to dream is to be aware only of images, without recognizing the images *as* images, hence without distinguishing them from their original. To dream is to be completely caught up with images, to be oblivious to those things of which they are images.

What, then, about the dream of the χώρα? What are the images in which we remain caught up? What are the distinctions to which we are blind?

In the dream, deprived by it of lucidity, we "affirm that it is necessary that all that is be somewhere in some place [τόπος] and occupy some χώρα". The word τόπος can of course be translated as *place*; one might presume even that it was partly because of this very passage that χώρα too came to be translated as *locus* (Calcidius) and then as *place* (Thomas Taylor). But in texts prior to the Aristotelian determination of τόπος it is more appropriate to render τόπος as something like *region*. Even Aristotle, though fixing a precise sense, still uses the word in this sense, dividing the entire universe into three τόποι.[17] What is operative in such division is the intrinsic connection made in Greek thought between specific regions and what, from Aristotle on (though not yet in Plato), are called the elements; the upper region is that of fire and aether, the lower that of earth. In fact, just after the chorology there is a passage that makes this connection explicit: "The greater part of each kind keeps apart in a region [τόπος] of its own because of the movement of the recipient" (57c). Thus, in failing to make the distinction between χώρα and τόπος, conflating them by mere coordination, as in the passage, one fails to distinguish between the χώρα and its appearance as, for instance, a fiery region.[18] In the dream one simply pictures the χώρα as a kind of region of regions in which all things would have their place. Hence, one conflates the χώρα and τόπος; one fails to distinguish between the χώρα and its appearance, even though this appearing is not a matter of casting an image. For in the *autre temps* of the χώρα there are no images, only traces of fire, air, water, and earth.

In the dream there is also an equally decisive conflation of the intelligible and the sensible, even though in the *autre temps* of the χώρα the sensible has still to become itself, that is, still consists only of fugitive traces. The dream vision is of a region in which all that is would be placed, whereas one who awakens from the dream will – as Timaeus goes on to say – recognize that the intelligible εἴδη are set apart, that they do not pass anywhere else into another. To awaken from the dream would be, then, to come to distinguish the three kinds conflated in the oneiric vision, to come to count them off in their distinctness, reenacting the opening words of the dialogue: *one, two, three*.

But in the dream something is received, as if conferred by some power of divination. Even though in the dream one fails to distinguish between the three kinds, still something is *disclosed* in the dream, namely, that of which one dreams, the χώρα. Furthermore, awakening from the dream, one can then draw those proper distinctions that were lacking in the oneiric vision: Timaeus demonstrates this in deed by going on to say the truth that one would say upon awakening, telling how it is that by virtue of the χώρα images, sensible things, first come to be[19] – to the extent that it can be told and to the extent that they come *to be* (rather than being nothing at all). Thus, he tells how the χώρα is the site where a new time begins, a time other than the *autre temps* of the χώρα. But he can tell of this time of images only by telling – if more distinctly – about the dream-image of that *autre temps* when there were yet no images but only the fugitive traces of things not yet themselves.

Much later in the dialogue Timaeus speaks of the liver. What he says makes it clear that the liver is a kind of reproduction of the χώρα within the human body. Timaeus says that it is made smooth and bright so that "the power of thoughts that proceed from intellect [νοῦς] move in the liver as in a mirror that receives impressions and provides visible images" (*Tim.* 71b). It is then around the liver that a part of the soul "in the night passes its time sensibly, being occupied in its slumbers with divination [μαντεία], since it does not partake of λόγος or φρόνησις (*Tim.* 71d). Thus, there is in the lower parts of soul and body an organ of divination, a gift that the god gave to man's foolishness. One undergoes divination only when one's intellect is fettered in sleep or distraught by disease or by divine inspiration (διά τινα ἐνθουσιασμόν). But, says Timaeus, "it belongs to a man when in his right senses [ἔμφρονος] to recollect and ponder the things spoken in dream or waking vision by the divining and inspired nature" (*Tim.* 71e).

Awakening to the light of day, Timaeus will thus have interpreted the dream, pondering it while still no doubt finding himself carried away by it, dreaming it again but now in daytime.

It is as if night, *l'autre nuit*, Hades itself, were to be drawn up into the light of day. One could not hope to do so except by also leaving it in the depth, keeping one's back to it, as Orpheus could hope to lead Eurydice out of Hades only by not looking back at her. Yet we know that Orpheus did not submit to this necessity: the moment he stepped out into daylight, he turned his gaze back upon her only to see her, because of his excessive act, slipping back into the darkness. This is, in the words of Blanchot, "an infinitely problematical movement, which the day condemns as unjustifiable madness"[20] – the madness of the day.

Can it be otherwise with a daydream? With a daydream of the χώρα?

Pennsylvania State University

Notes

[1] Jacques Derrida, "Tense", trans. D.F. Krell, in *The Path of Archaic Thinking: Unfolding the Work of John Sallis*, ed. Kenneth Maly (Albany: State University of New York Press, 1995), 73. The present text may be read as continuing a discussion that began with a brief presentation I gave at Cerisy-la-Salle in 1992. The presentation was oriented to Derrida's *Khôra* (Paris: Galilée, 1993), which appeared in the first version in *Poikilia. Études offertes à Jean-Pierre Vernant* (Paris: EHESS, 1987) and in an English translation by Ian McLeod in *On the Name* (Stanford: Stanford University Press, 1995). My presentation has appeared in French ("De la Chôra", in *Le passage des frontières: Autour du travail de Jacques Derrida* [Paris: Galilée, 1994]) and in English ("Of the Χώρα", *Epoché* II/1 (1994): 1–12). Derrida takes up and extends the discussion in "Tense", especially pp. 70–74, together with note 11 (p. 284), which refers to "De la Chôra".

[2] Ibid., 49.
[3] Ibid.
[4] Derrida, "Avances", preceding: Serge Margel, *Le Tombeau du Dieu Artisan* (Paris: Les Éditions de Minuit, 1995), 12.
[5] Martin Heidegger, *Sein und Zeit* (Tübingen: Max Niemeyer Verlag, 1960), 413.
[6] Maurice Blanchot, *L'Espace Littéraire* (Paris: Gallimard, 1955), 222.
[7] Derrida, *Khôra*, 21.
[8] Samuel Beckett, *Collected Shorter Prose 1945–1980* (London: John Calder, 1984), 145–147.
[9] Derrida, *Khôra*, 28.
[10] In a more recent text Derrida seems to insist even on this translation, though surrounding it with precautions and exclusions that serve to ward off many of the ghosts that otherwise would haunt it so incessantly as to make the word χώρα, as it operates in the *Timaeus*, virtually unreadable in a word such as *lieu*. Still: "*Khôra* ... would be, at least according to the interpretation that I have ventured of it, the name of place [*le nom de lieu*],

a name of place ..." ("Foi et savoir: Les deux sources de la 'religion' aux limites de la simple raison", in *La Religion* [Séminaire de Capri sous la direction de Jacques Derrida et Gianni Vattimo] [Paris: Éditions du Seuil, 1996], 31).

[11] Ibid.
[12] Derrida, "Tense", 73.
[13] Derrida, "Foi et savoir", 31.
[14] I have discussed these passages of the *Republic* in detail in *Being and Logos: Reading the Platonic Dialogues*, 3rd ed. (Bloomington: Indiana University Press, 1996), 401–443.
[15] See my discussion in *Delimitations: Phenomenoloy and the End of Metaphysics*, 2nd ed. (Bloomington: Indiana University Press, 1995), chap. 1.
[16] Derrida, *Khôra*, 17.
[17] Aristotle, Progression of Animals 706b.
[18] Just before the chorology Timaeus speaks of the peculiar appearing of the χώρα: "That part of it that is made fiery appears as fire" (*Tim.* 51b). Immediately following the chorology there is another, similar reference to such appearing (see *Tim.* 52d–e). My text "Of the Χώρα" is largely oriented to the question of this appearing.
[19] See my discussion in "Of the Χώρα", 7–9.
[20] Blanchot, *L'Espace littéraire*, 229. See also *La folie du jour* (Fata morgana, 1973) and Derrida's related text "La loi du genre", in *Parages* (Paris: Galilée, 1986), 249–287.

Chapter 5

Deconstruction, Ontology, and Philosophy of Science: Derrida on Aristotle

Christopher Norris

Ontological Relativity Revisited

Jacques Derrida's essay 'The Supplement of Copula' contains some of the most detailed and convincing *anti*-relativist arguments to be found anywhere in the recent philosophic literature.[1] I have stated the case thus baldly – and italicized the crucial prefix – since my claim is likely to conjure scepticism (or outright disbelief) among many readers. After all, it is well known that Derrida espouses an extreme version of the current Nietzschean/poststructuralist *doxa* according to which 'truth' and 'reality' are wholly linguistic (or textual) constructs. Moreover we have it on good authority – not only from hostile sources but also from admiring commentators such as Richard Rorty – that Derrida subscribes to a range of kindred anti-realist and cultural-relativist beliefs.[2] On a quick reckoning these include: (1) the Nietzsche-inspired thesis that 'all concepts are sublimated metaphors', all truth-claims a species of rhetorical imposition; (2) the idea of philosophical discourse as just another 'kind of writing', on a par with poetry, fiction, or literary criticism; (3) the refusal to privilege philosophy as in any sense a constructive, truth-seeking, or problem-solving activity; (4) the deconstruction of Western ('logocentric') metaphysics as a source of these and other such self-deluding hopes; and (5) the proposal that we throw off the constraints of that old (now bankrupt) dispensation and learn to enjoy the freedoms opened up for a 'post-philosophical' culture where thinking (or writing) is no longer subject to the grim paternal law of reality and truth.

No matter that Derrida has gone out of his way to reject or disown items (1) to (5) above – along with a range of kindred *idées reçues* – as bearing not the least resemblance to anything he has written during three decades of immensely productive authorship.[3] No matter that they owe more to hearsay than to first-hand acquaintance with his texts, having gained currency chiefly through the influence of Rorty's oft-cited essay 'Philosophy as a Kind of Writing'.[4] For this is what many Anglo-American philosophers want to think about Derrida, representing as he does a convenient target in the current round of renewed inter-faculty ('philosophy versus literary theory') and intercultural ('analytic' versus 'Continental') sectarian strife. My main purpose here is to challenge this widespread and damaging misperception of Derrida's work. But I shall also argue that certain of his texts – notably 'The Supplement of Copula' and 'White Mythology' – have a strong and distinctive contribution to make in the context of recent analytical debate. More specifically: they offer an alternative approach to issues of truth, meaning, and interpretation that have driven some philosophers – Stephen Schiffer among them – to despair of achieving any further constructive advance.[5] Then again there is Donald Davidson's conspicuous retreat from a truth-based (Tarskian) semantics intended as an argument against various forms of cultural and linguistic relativism to a position where truth pretty much drops out, where utterer's meaning can only be construed on the basis of some ad hoc 'passing theory' adopted in this or that communicative context, and where 'wit, luck, and wisdom' are the best we have to go on in figuring out each other's intentions.[6] Thus, according to Davidson, there is 'no such thing as a language' if by 'language' is meant what philosophers and linguists have usually understood by that term. And there is no such thing as defining the conditions for adequate intra- or inter-linguistic understanding if those conditions are thought to entail something more than a localized, chance convergence on some 'theory' arrived at by intuitive guesswork.

Davidson nevertheless remains quite sanguine about the prospects for our everyday, practical communicative grasp, in contrast to Schiffer who is hard put to explain why his argument is neither 'defeatist' nor 'despairing'. At any rate they both now occupy the sort of 'post-analytic' position that Rorty can welcome as yet another pointer to philosophy's decently scaled-down role in the 'cultural conversation of mankind'.[7] Moreover, they are united in no longer seeing any hope for a strong truth-conditional theory – in Schiffer's case, a theory of belief-based propositional semantics – that would counter the sceptical-relativist trend. It is against this background of failed endeavour in a certain branch of the analytic enterprise (more specifically: of logical empiricism and various successor movements) that I shall here focus on Derrida's approach to a range of kindred topics.

Of course I am not the first to attempt such a bridge-building exercise. There are, for instance, well-versed commentators who perceive a close affinity between Derrida's treatment of issues in Austinian speech-act theory and Davidson's late (minimalist-semantic) approach to meaning and interpretation.[8] Thus they have each come around – so the argument runs – to a broadly pragmatic or holistic view according to which there can exist no necessary and sufficient criteria – much less any generalized theory – as regards what shall count as a proper intention or a validating context for genuine ('felicitous') speech-act utterance. On this view there is no great difference between Derrida's talk of speech-act 'iterability' – the capacity of performatives to function across a vast (potentially limitless) range of contexts – and Davidson's notion of 'passing theories' as likewise all that is required in order to explain how people manage to communicate from one context to the next.[9] However, the purpose of these comparisons is usually to argue for the kind of entente cordiale that would bring Derrida out on the side of recent developments in 'post-analytic' philosophy. That is to say, they would treat him as having travelled much the same path – and to much the same sceptical terminus – as thinkers like Davidson and Schiffer. It seems to me that this gets Derrida wrong as regards both his reading of Austin and his general approach to issues in the area of truth, meaning, and interpretation. Worst of all it ignores what his work has to offer by way of counter-argument to the presently widespread cultural-relativist trend.

Derrida on Benveniste

In 'The Supplement of Copula' Derrida takes issue with some claims advanced by the linguist Emile Benveniste concerning Aristotle's doctrine of the categories or modes of predicative judgement.[10] According to Benveniste these had their origin in a certain natural language (the ancient Greek) whose lexical resources and grammatical structures are everywhere drawn upon in Aristotle's quasi-universalist mode of argument.[11] Thus: 'Aristotle, reasoning in the absolute, is simply identifying certain fundamental categories of the language in which he thought'.[12] And the same would apply to those thinkers after Aristotle (Kant among them) who criticized his table of the categories but who sought to overcome its limitations through a further, more rigorous exercise of reason. For in their case also, as Benveniste contends, there is a failure to grasp that any such claim must rest upon this unconscious transfer of attributes from language to the putative laws of thought or a priori conditions for valid reasoning.

Nor is it in any way remarkable that this certain 'small document' (Benveniste's phrase) concerning the categories should have come to exert such an influence not only on later philosophical thought but across a wide range of cognate disciplines, linguistics and philology included. For those disciplines have themselves grown up within the matrix of various natural languages that exhibit a close kinship with the ancient Greek in respect of both their lexico-grammatical structures and – as follows necessarily on Benveniste's account – their associated range of logico-semantic or predicative functions. Thus: 'while granting absolutely that thought cannot be grasped except as formed and made a reality in language, have we any means to recognize in thought such characteristics as would belong to it alone and owe nothing to linguistic expression?'[13] For Benveniste this question is purely rhetorical since it posits a thesis (the existence of language-independent structures of thought) whose impossibility is granted in the opening clause. After all, such a thesis would have to be expressed – to achieve articulate form – in one or another natural language whose surface (grammatical) features were assumed to reflect, embody, or exemplify its deeper (logical) structure. But there could then be no possible argument to establish the priority of 'thought' over 'language', or – as Benveniste tends to view the issue – of 'philosophy' over 'linguistics'. For such an argument would always be constrained to ignore the fact of its own dependence upon language as the precondition for expressing any claim whatsoever with regard to this thesis.

Rather than summarize Derrida's lengthy and complex response, I shall begin by examining one crucial passage from 'The Supplement of Copula'. It is devoted to a single sentence in Benveniste's text, the only place – so Derrida maintains – where the issue comes clearly (if not perhaps consciously) into focus. This question of consciousness is crucial to his argument since it is Benveniste's claim that Aristotle, in his treatment of the categories, was unconscious of the fact that these supposedly absolute (non-language-relative) necessities of thought were themselves the product of a merely contingent, 'empirical' set of lexico-grammatical constraints pertaining to the Greek language. Thus Benveniste: 'Unconsciously he [Aristotle] took as a criterion the empirical necessity of a distinct expression for each of his predications'.[14] But what can 'empirical' mean here? Derrida asks. 'Taken literally, this explanation would suppose that Aristotle, having at his disposition, moreover, and outside of language, predicates, or conceivable classes of predicates, and faced with the empirical necessity of expressing these contents ... confused the distinction of predicates and the distinction of expressions'. ('Supplement of Copula', p. 190)

In short, Benveniste is here invoking a range of categorical distinctions, as between 'empirical' and 'conceivable' orders of thought, or natural-language expressions on the one hand and, on the other, those classes of predicates 'outside of language' whose very possibility he seeks to deny. Thus:

> Is it not strange to qualify as empirical the necessity of an expression, the necessity to bring the conceivable to statement in a given language? In the last analysis, the value of empiricity has never been related to anything but the variability of sensory and individual givens, and by extension to every passivity or activity without concept ... Above all, how can one affirm the empiricity of the movement which leads to signifying in general and to signifying within a language, and that does so with recourse to an organization of forms, a distribution of classes, etc.? Finally, on the basis of what system, and also from whence historically, do we receive and understand – before even positing the empiricity of signification – the signification of empiricity? On this matter no analysis will either circumvent or exclude the tribunal of Aristotelianism. This does not imply that Aristotle is the author or origin of the concept of empiricity, even if the opposition of the empirical and the theoretical (the *a priori*, the scientific, the objective, the systematic, etc.) in one way or another envelops Aristotle's metaphysics. Even if such a concept is not fixed once and for all in an 'origin', one cannot comprehend the history and system of its mutations or transformations without taking into account the general code of metaphysics, and within this code, the decisive mark of Aristotelianism. (p. 192)

This passage evokes a whole range of related issues within current analytic (or 'post-analytic') philosophy, issues which have struck some commentators (Schiffer among them) as beyond hope of adequate treatment.[15] It also exemplifies the distinctive mode of transcendental argument – reasoning from the conditions of possibility for thought about truth, meaning, and interpretation – that plays such a prominent role in Derrida's earlier writings.[16] Thus my aim in what follows is to suggest a more promising way forward from the post-analytical fix to which, as it seems, the only solutions are either (1) an all-but avowedly 'defeatist' outlook like Schiffer's, (2) the Davidsonian recourse to meaning-holism or minimalist semantics as a 'theory to end all theories', or (3) a Rortian neopragmatist approach that comes out (supposedly) on the far side of all that misguided 'metaphysical' or truth-fixated talk. At least there is a case for suspending those habits of ingrained prejudice that have so far prevented most analytic philosophers from attending seriously to Derrida's work.

I shall now return to the above-cited passage from 'The Supplement of Copula' where Derrida examines the difficulties encountered with Benveniste's reading of Aristotle. For that passage has an obvious bearing on the problems of logical empiricism and the subsequent history of likewise problematical attempts to escape such an overly rigid dualism of empirical matters-of-fact on the one hand and conceptual truths-of-reason on the other. This history is familiar enough, from Quine's 'Two Dogmas of Empiricism' to the various present-day schools of thought which endorse ontological relativity and meaning-holism as the only means of avoiding that particular philosophical dead-end.[17] And from here it is a short distance to those post-analytical viewpoints – whether sadly disillusioned like Schiffer's or vaguely hopeful like Davidson's – which give up the attempt to specify truth-conditions or criteria for meaningful utterance beyond those provided by a pragmatist appeal to what is 'good in the way of belief'. That Schiffer still professes to find this outcome deeply disturbing bears witness more to the strength of his residual analytic attachment than to anything in his theory – or what little now remains of it – that could offer a genuine or workable alternative. Hence Rorty's confident prediction that all these thinkers must at last come around to a pragmatist view of philosophy's role as just one more (strictly non-privileged) participant voice in the 'cultural conversation of mankind'.

Derrida is often cited – by disciples and detractors alike – as a thinker who has pushed a long way in the direction of mininalist semantics, meaning-holism, ontological relativity, and suchlike (currently fashionable) doctrines.[18] However, the above passage should be enough to discountenance any reading of his work that entertains this mistaken view. What it brings out very clearly is Derrida's refusal of that reductive logical-empiricist approach together with the various alternatives proposed by post-analytical philosophers. Thus when Derrida remarks – as against Benveniste – that '[o]n this matter no analysis will either circumvent or exclude the tribunal of Aristotelianism', his comment has a relevance to issues beyond the particular case in hand. It is best understood in connection with his other main points about the relationship between 'conscious' and 'unconscious' elements in the discourse of (or on) philosophy and the 'value of empiricity' as that which 'has never been related to anything but the variability of sensory and individual givens, and by extension to every passivity or activity without concept' ('Supplement of Copula', p. 192). For it is precisely this latter assumption that finds its most dogmatic (uncritical) expression in the doctrine of logical empiricism, that is, the intransigent dichotomy between matters of fact or empirical warrant and truths-of-reason or those whose validity is a matter of purely definitional (analytic) self-evidence. And this connects in turn with Benveniste's charge against Aristotle: that he remained 'unconcious' of those empirical elements in his own thinking – namely the contingent lexico-grammatical resources of the Greek language – which he mistook for categorical necessities pertaining to language and thought in general. Thus, according to Benveniste, 'unconsciously and without wanting to, he [Aristotle] has taken the "class of forms", such as the system of language offers it, for the system of the expressed or the expressible' ('Supplement of Copula', p. 190). But as Derrida shows, this charge applies more aptly to Benveniste himself, resorting as he does – at whatever "unconscious" or involuntary level – to various strictly categorical distinctions (like those between thought and language, conscious and unconscious, the conceptual and the empirical, the 'distinction of predicates' and the 'distinction of expressions') without which he could not have advanced a single proposition on this topic. All of which suggests that there is 'in the practice of a language, in the belonging to a language, a structural necessity for this "unconscious" to be produced, such that what is pointed out in Aristotle would be but the confirmation of the general law of unconsciousness' (p. 190).

As should hardly need saying this 'unconsciousness' has nothing to do with a Freudian or depth-psychological account of sublimated motives and desires. It is a 'structural necessity' in the Kantian sense that the conditions of possibility for knowledge – both for self-knowledge and epistemological enquiry – are such as must always remain in some degree opaque or resistant to the philosophic quest for clear and distinct ideas. Indeed, some of Derrida's most closely-argued analytical work – including his several early books on Husserl – is devoted to uncovering the blind-spots, the structural limits or aporias encountered by philosophy in its repeated attempts to make good on that Cartesian ambition.[19] But this does not lead him, as it does Rorty, to dismiss the entire enterprise as an ultimately failed or useless endeavour, a project hung up on certain otiose metaphors – like the mind as a 'mirror of nature' – which philosophers have taken as a pretext for vainly attempting to explain how it is that our language 'matches up' with the world through this or that currently favoured candidate-theory.[20] On the contrary, Derrida insists that such notions of simply 'turning the page' on philosophy as hitherto practised always amount to just 'philosophizing badly' or in ignorance of questions – such as those raised in Benveniste's reading of Aristotle – whose out-of-hand dismissal opens the way to all manner of naive or uncritical prejudice.[21] (One is reminded of J.M. Keynes's canny remark that those who profess to have no 'theory' are usually working on a bad old theory which they can't or won't acknowledge.) For there is a difference – a crucial difference – between that order of 'structural' unconsciousness which attends even the most critical or reflective exercise of thought and, on the other hand, that demonstrable lack of awareness (the phrase seems more appropriate here) which leads Benveniste to charge Aristotle with 'unconsciously' mistaking some empirical facts about the Greek language for categorical necessities of thought. As Derrida puts it: '[i]f one wished to use the word 'empirical' in a sense totally foreign to Aristotle's, or to its sense in the history of philosophy, one explicitly would have to undertake the labour of this transformation. Nothing in Benveniste's text signals or announces such a displacement' ('Supplement of Copula', p. 192).

Derrida's point is that the word 'empirical' cannot be used in a sense 'totally foreign' to Aristotle's, any more than thinking could be carried on – as Benveniste purports to show – in a language that dispensed altogether with the Aristotelian categories, and which thus showed them up as a merely 'empirical' (since language-dependent) artefact. What is none the less possible, Derrida suggests, is a certain specific 'labour of transformation' through which empiricism may acquire a different, perhaps a more productive (causal or depth-explanatory) yield, and through which those categories may themselves be subject to a process of ongoing criticism, refinement, and modification. It is precisely this possibility that Derrida explores in some pages of his essay 'White Mythology: metaphor in the text of philosophy' devoted to Bachelard's and Canguilhem's work on the role of metaphor in scientific discourse and its 'rectification' by way of more advanced (conceptual and empirical) research.[22] Nothing could be further from the Rortian idea that science – like philosophy – comes down to just a series of optative metaphors or periodic shifts in the kinds of language-game that set the agenda for current debate.[23]

It might seem merely perverse on my part to present Derrida as a transcendental realist, one who comes out in agreement with philosophers of science like Roy Bhaskar in seeking to maintain the vital distinction between ontological and epistemological issues.[24] In fact one could instance quite a number of passages, especially from recent interviews, where Derrida protests against the widespread misreading of his work that has taken certain sentences out of context (most notoriously, 'il n'y a pas de hors-texte': 'there is no "outside" to the text') and used them to portray him as some sort of far-gone transcendental idealist.[25] Still, it might be said that these passages are part of a rearguard defensive campaign and should therefore not be granted any special credence merely on account of their outraged tone. More to the point is the evidence of those earlier texts – 'White Mythology' and 'The Supplement of Copula' among them – which cannot be read in that fashion unless by a very determined effort to suppress or distort large portions of Derrida's argument. What they bring out rather is the impossibility (the 'rigorous and principled' impossibility) of relativizing thought to language as Benveniste would have it, or of treating concepts – scientific or philosophical concepts – as so many repressed, forgotten, or sublimated metaphors, entirely on a par as regards their delusory truth-content.

Thus there is simply no way that the relativist case can be propounded without running into the kinds of performative and logical contradiction that Derrida detects in Benveniste's reading of Aristotle. And the same would apply to any version of the wholesale anti-realist doctrine which urges – most often with reference to Nietzsche – that we abandon the old 'metaphysical' idea of a real world whose objects, processes, and events are to be thought of as existing independently of our own (arbitrarily-imposed) categories, language-games, social constructions, conceptual schemes, metaphorical preferences, and so forth.[26] This reading of Nietzsche is itself highly questionable, given his express desire to distinguish between *Wissenschaft* as a genuinely truth-seeking enterprise and those various pseudo-sciences that merely adopt a rhetoric of truth as a means to dissimulate their own power-seeking interests.[27] But even taking Nietzsche on the terms favoured by his current post-structuralist disciples – that is, as an all-out epistemological sceptic – there still remains the question of whether such a doctrine is intelligible as construed from his own texts or as applied to issues in those various related fields (epistemology, philosophy of language, history and philosophy of science) where its consequences would have the most decisive and unsettling impact. It is in this context that Derrida turns to Bachelard and Canguilhem for a series of well-documented cases where scientific enquiry can be shown to have started out from some image-complex or metaphorical quasi-concept, but then to have advanced through a process of critical 'rectification' which made it possible to allow and discount for those residues of anthropomorphic thinking.[28]

Canguilhem cites a very pertinent passage from Bichat's *Treatise on Membranes* (1880):

> The term 'tissue' deserves to give us pause. Tissue comes, as is well known, from *tistre*, an archaic form of the verb *tisser*, to weave. If the word 'cell' has appeared to be overburdened with implicit significations of an affective and social order, the word 'tissue' appears no less burdened with extra-theoretical implications. 'Cell' makes us think of the bee, and not of man. 'Tissue' makes us think of man, and not of the spider. Tissue, a weave, is the human product *par excellence*.[29]

Of course there is a sense in which scientific discourse cannot do without metaphor, that is, without resorting to figures of thought which enable some analogy to be drawn between familiar modes of knowledge or perception and novel (as yet inadequately theorized) domains of research. This is why Derrida questions the idea of conceptual 'rectification' in so far as it might be taken to imply that science could pass altogether beyond the realm of metaphorical expression into a realm of clear and distinct concepts redeemed from such archaic or primitive residues. Thus 'clear' and 'distinct' are themselves metaphorical terms, along with many others – 'idea' and 'theory' among them – whose sense points back (chiefly via Descartes) to the Greek association between accurate conceptual knowledge and accurate visual or ocular representation. 'Concept' is another such metaphor, this time drawn from the tactile range – 'grasping together', as of complex ideas in a single act of thought – whose members would include such cognate words as 'grasp' and 'comprehension'. So there is reason enough for Derrida's doubt that this process of epistemo-critical 'rectification' must always move 'from metaphor to concept' in a linear or smoothly progressivist fashion, or (another version of the same idea) that 'tropes must necessarily belong to the prescientific phase of thought'.[30]

However, he is just as far from endorsing the opposite – currently widespread – fallacy which rejects the very notions of scientific truth, knowledge, or progress on account of their belonging to that sheerly rhetorical will-to-power that Nietzsche was the first to diagnose and which Derrida (supposedly) has 'deconstructed' to the point where only a naive realist could find them in the least degree plausible.[31] After all, as Derrida very pertinently remarks, 'there is also a concept of metaphor: it too has a history, yields knowledge, demands from the epistemologist construction, rectification, critical rules of importation and exportation' ('White Mythology', p. 224). More than that: there could be no accounting either for science or the history and philosophy of science were it not for (1) the existence of a real-world, mind-independent domain of which knowledge is nonetheless attainable; (2) the capacity to 'rectify' naive or hitherto unnoticed metaphors, analogies, anthropomorphisms, etc.; and (3) the resultant possibility of advancing 'from an inefficient tropic-concept that is poorly constructed, to an operative tropic-concept that is more refined and more powerful in a given field and at a determined phase of the scientific process' (p. 264). It would, I acknowledge, be somewhat absurd to present Derrida as a full-fledged scientific realist seeking to refute any version of that sceptical-relativist doctrine whose sources include Nietzsche, Saussure, and – as rumour would have it – Derrida himself. But it is equally the case that this orthodoxy rests on a partial and distorted reading of his texts and one that is demonstrably wide of the mark when set against the relevant passages in 'White Mythology' and 'The Supplement of Copula'.

Still, beyond that, there is the prior question as to whether such doctrines are scientifically and philosophically justified, quite aside from the issue of exegetical fidelity to Nietzsche's or (indeed) to Derrida's text. I would argue that a realist and causal-explanatory approach is alone among present-day candidate-theories in offering an adequate response to items (1) to (3) in the above list of desiderata. Most importantly, it insists upon respecting the difference – the *ontological* difference though not (I should stress) in anything like Heidegger's sense – between the order of real-world (physically instantiated) objects, process and events and the order of conceptual-explanatory thought that affords our best current knowledge regarding that ontic domain. For a great deal of the confusion that surrounds this issue of scientific truth can be seen as resulting from a failure to observe what is surely one of the most basic lessons of all human thought and experience. Bertrand Russell made much the same point – and with similar relativist doctrines in view – in a typically vigorous and plain-speaking passage from his 1912 book *The Problems of Philosophy*.

> Minds do not create truth or falsehood. They create beliefs, but when once the beliefs are created, the mind cannot make them true or false, except in the special case where they concern future things which are within the power of the person believing, such as catching trains. What makes a belief true is a fact, and and this fact does not (except in exceptional cases) in any way involve the mind of the person who has the belief.[32]

For 'mind' and 'belief' read 'language-game', 'discourse', 'text', 'paradigm', 'conceptual scheme', or cultural 'form of life' – in short, all the various substitute-terms that are nowadays common coin among relativist thinkers who have taken the 'linguistic turn' after Nietzsche, Saussure, Foucault, late Witttgenstein, or (as these exegetes are fond of putting it) 'a certain' Derrida.[33] What they share is a total rejection of Russell's argument that truth may indeed be 'relative', but relative precisely to those real-world (mind-independent) states of affairs that determine what shall count as a veridical belief.

Let us once again take Benveniste as an advocate for the relativist view, albeit a linguist of immense erudition who advances his case – unlike so many of the above company – through a highly detailed and articulate process of critical argument. 'Now it seems to us', Benveniste writes, 'that these distinctions are primarily categories of language and that, in fact, Aristotle, reasoning in the absolute, is simply identifying certain fundamental categories of the language in which he thought'.[34] And again:

> this language has a configuration in all its parts and as a totality. It is in addition organized as an arrangement of distinct and distinguishing 'signs', capable themselves of being broken down into interior units or of being grouped into complex units. This great structure, which includes substructures of several levels, gives its form to the content of thought.[35]

What we recognise in this passage – expressed with great clarity and precision – is the structuralist model of language (*la langue*) conceived under its synchronic aspect as a system of interdependent relationships and differences, a network or economy of signifying elements hierarchically ordered for the purpose of more adequate conceptualization.[36] Whatever his criticisms of it elsewhere that project is one that Derrida has often acknowledged as a crucial and indeed a formative influence on his own thinking. That 'a certain structuralism has always been philosophy's most spontaneous gesture' – as he cryptically declared in one early essay – is by no means to be taken as a wholly negative verdict on either structuralism or philosophy.[37]

Nevertheless, there are problems about Benveniste's confident extension of the structuralist programme to a point where it claims to establish a priori the precedence of 'language' over 'thought', or – in more narrowly disciplinary terms – of linguistics over philosophy. For as Derrida pointedly remarks:

> The notion of a linguistic system, even if opposed to the notions of logical system, or system of categories, and even if one attempted to reduce the latter to the former, would never have been possible outside the history (and) of the concepts of metaphysics as theory, *episteme*, etc. Whatever the displacements, breaks, and secondary discontinuities of every kind (and they surely have to be taken very strictly into account), this affiliation has never been absolutely interrupted. ('Supplement of Copula', p. 180)

This argument is precisely analogous to Derrida's point about the relationship between concept and metaphor: that any simple (quasi-Nietzschean) attempt to invert their received 'logocentric' order of priority will always have recourse to a philosophic schema that has already provided the working definition of both those cardinal terms. Moreover, it is from Aristotle's fourth (and 'best') type of metaphor – the type that operates through proportion-schemes or complex analogies of the form 'A is to B as C is to D' – that most subsequent discussions have taken their lead.

The best-known statement of this theory is that which appears in the *Poetics*, but it is also implicit – as Derrida remarks – in a great many passages from Aristotle's texts on rhetoric, linguistics, interpretation-theory, metaphysics, ontology, and the natural sciences. In its canonical version:

> Metaphor (*metaphora*) consists in giving (*epiphora*) the thing a name (*onomatos*) that belongs to something else (*allotriou*), the transference being either from genus to species (*apo tou genous eidos*), or from species to genus (*apo tou eidous epi to genos*), or from species to species (*apo tou eidous epi eidos*), or on the grounds of analogy. (*e kata to analogon*)[38]

Derrida makes two (apparently contradictory) points about this passage. On the one hand 'it is a philosophical thesis about metaphor', a thesis that occupies its proper place within the 'great immobile chain' of Aristotelian ontology whose structure comprehends the entire range of natural and human sciences. Thus it belongs to a system of interpretation where metaphor is construed (in Derrida's words) as a 'provisional loss of meaning, an economy of the proper without irreparable damage' ('White Mythology', p. 270). On the other hand it is also 'a philosophical discourse whose entire surface is worked by a metaphorics' (p. 232). That is to say, Aristotle's definition of the various types of metaphor – his attempt to specify just how they depart from the proper or literal norm – itself has recourse to a range of figural expressions (metaphors of movement, transfer, kinship, biological species and genera) which bear the main burden of his argument. As might be expected, given that the very term 'metaphor' derives from the Greek verb *metapherein* ('to carry across'), thus suggesting the transfer of sense by analogy from one term to another and constituting an instance of catachresis, that is, a metaphorical expression for which there exists no literal equivalent. Moreover, *literal* is likewise catachrestic since its meaning – what is nowadays its 'literal' meaning – goes back to the idea that one can somehow establish the proper (non-metaphoric) sense of a word by attending closely to the letter rather than the spirit or the gist of what is written.

So one can see why Derrida describes the above passage from Aristotle as a discourse 'whose entire surface is worked by a metaphorics'. Still it is unwise to follow those readers of 'White Mythology' – literary theorists for the most part – who opt for the giddying *mise-en-abîme* that opens up (or so they think) on the far side of the concept–metaphor distinction.[39] I have noted already that Derrida provides plentiful cautions against such a reading, arguments in the strictly transcendental mode which demonstrate the impossibility of holding (or consistently maintaining) this pseudo-deconstructive view-from-nowhere.[40] Still it would be just as myopic to ignore those many and better-known passages in the essay which have offered a pretext for blanket declarations of the type: 'all concepts are metaphors', 'all truth-claims a species of fiction', 'all philosophy a "kind of writing"', and so forth. Thus for instance: 'there is no properly philosophical category to qualify a certain number of tropes that have conditioned the so-called "fundamental", "structuring", "original" philosophical oppositions; they are so many "metaphors" that would constitute the rubrics of such a tropology, the words "turn" or "trope" or "metaphor" being no exception to this rule' ('White Mythology', p. 229). However, one must set against this Derrida's equally insistent reminders that any such radical-sounding thesis on metaphor will itself take for granted much of what Aristotle had to say on this topic, even (or especially) where it seeks to overturn that entire 'logocentric' tradition of thought that has subordinated metaphor to concept.

Clearly Derrida is in some sense 'paraphrasing' Aristotle – not propounding a thesis of his own – when he writes: '[t]he condition for metaphor (for good and true metaphor) is the condition for truth' (p. 237). Or again, that 'metaphor, as an effect of *mimesis* and *homoiosis*, the manifestation of analogy, will be a means of knowledge, a means that is subordinate, but certain' (p. 238). Yet neither can these passages be simply set aside in favour of a reading that takes the text at its word when the theme is that of philosophy's ultimate undoing through metaphor, its powerlessness to contain or control its own metaphorical productions. For one will still have to reckon with the demonstrable truth that '[t]he concept of metaphor, along with all the predicates that allow its ordered extension and comprehension, is a philosopheme' (p. 228). Here at least Derrida may be taken as writing in the assertoric mode, presenting a case that is rigorously borne out by the entire structure and logic of his argument in 'White Mythology'. And one should bear this in mind when one encounters other, more ambivalent passages where the issue of attribution (crudely speaking: Aristotle or Derrida?) is harder to decide. Thus:

> A noun is proper when it has but a single sense. Better, it is only in this case that it is properly a noun. Univocity is the essence, or better, the *telos* of language. No philosophy, as such, has ever renounced this Aristotelian ideal. This ideal is philosophy Each time that polysemia is irreducible, when no unity of meaning is even promised to it, one is outside language. And consequently, outside humanity. (pp. 247–8)

There is a possible reading of this passage – say a composite Nietzschean–Heideggerian–poststructuralist–neopragmatist reading – that would have no difficulty in deciding the issue. To the extent that philosophy has pursued such ideals (truth, proper meaning, univocity, clear and distinct ideas, the 'rectifying' movement from 'bad' to 'good' metaphors, from *doxa* to *episteme*, from nominal to real essences, and so forth) it has always been embarked upon a hopeless quest and one that Derrida does well to renounce. Furthermore, if this leads 'outside language' and even (in some sense) 'outside humanity' then the price is still worth paying since we are thereby encouraged – as Rorty would argue – to explore more varied and inventive possibilities of metaphorical self-redescription.

Metaphor, Truth, and Ontology

I hope I have said enough to indicate what is wrong with all this, not only as a reading of Derrida but also as an argument on its own account. For those standards of assessment are in no way distinct, as tends to be assumed by hostile commentators who accuse him of mischievously blurring the line between 'genuine' philosophical argument and textual close-reading in the 'literary' mode.[41] This ignores the clear insistence on Derrida's part that getting things right through rigorous attentiveness to the texts of (say) Aristotle and Benveniste, even if it means controverting some of their express philosophical theses, is also – and inseparably – the means of arriving at a more adequate philosophical grasp of issues in ontology, epistemology, and philosophy of language. Thus it is the virtue of Benveniste's essay, as Derrida reads it, to raise the question of the relationship (the order of priority) between 'thought' and 'language' to a point where that question is susceptible of treatment in terms that involve nothing less than the *truth or falsehood* of Benveniste's proposal as a matter of demonstrative argument. What Benveniste 'discovers' – despite and against his overt linguistic-relativist claims – is 'the absolutely unique relationship between the transcendental and language', taking the term transcendental 'in its most rigorously accepted sense, in its most avowed "technicalness", precisely as it was fixed in the course of the development of the Aristotelian problematic of the categories' ('Supplement of Copula', p. 195). And that development would include not only Aristotle's discussion but also, for instance, Kant's attempt to establish his own (somewhat modified) doctrine of the categories on the basis of an argument from the conditions of possibility for thought and judgment in general.[42]

It may be said – and quite rightly – that Derrida evinces a high degree of scepticism with regard to such claims, or at any rate a refusal to accept them as a priori valid on the terms and conditions laid down by philosophers from Aristotle to Kant and Husserl.[43] But it would none the less be wrong to conclude that he regards this whole enterprise as inherently deluded or (after Nietzsche) as the 'history of an error', that which consists in mistaking metaphors for concepts, or in failing to perceive how all our concepts, categories, and truth-claims are merely the products of an epistemic will-to-power and a consequent need to repress or dissimulate their own rhetorical constitution.[44] For it is just this argument – albeit proposed in more moderate form – that also finds expression in Benveniste's claim for the priority of 'language' over 'thought' and hence (implicitly) of linguistics over philosophy as the discipline best qualified to establish that fact. 'What is not examined at any time', Derrida writes, 'is the common category of the category, the categoriality in general on the basis of which the categories of language and the categories of thought may be dissociated' ('Supplement of Copula', p. 182). Moreover, it can be shown that this concept 'systematically comes into play in the history of philosophy and of science (in Aristotle's *Organon* and *Categories*) at the point where the opposition of language to thought is impossible, or has only a very derivative sense' (ibid.). So the issue of priority between thought and language cannot even be raised – or intelligibly discussed – in terms which take that opposition for granted without enquiring further into its own (strictly prior) metaphysical or conceptual conditions of possibility.

All of which requires that any adequate address to this topic will have to start out from that passage in Aristotle's *Metaphysics* where his listing of the categories is preceded by what Derrida calls 'a kind of principial definition', one that presents them as an answer to the question 'of knowing in what ways Being is said, since it is said *pollakos*, in many ways'. This science, Aristotle argues,

> will be prior to physics, and will be primary philosophy and universal in this sense, that it is primary. And it will be the province of this science to study Being *qua* Being; what it is (*ti esti*), and what the attributes are which belong to it *qua* Being. But the simple term 'being' (*to haplos legomenon*; *Haplos*: simply, frankly, in a word, without detour) is used in various senses (*pollakos legetai*), of which we saw that one was accidental (*kata sumbebekos*) and another true (*os alethes*), not-being being used in the sense of false (*kai to me on os to pseudos*); and besides these there are the categories (*ta skhemata tes kategorias*), for example the 'what' (*ti*), quality (*poion*), quantity (*poson*), place (*pou*), time (*pote*), and any other meanings.[45]

Interpretations of Aristotle nowadays divide into two sharply opposed readings of this and other passages like it. On the one hand is that Heideggerian interpretation which treats Aristotle as having raised the primordial 'question of Being' – of a 'science' that would precede physics, metaphysics, and all such merely 'ontic' or 'factical' concerns – but as falling back into a mode of epistemological (subject-based representationalist) thought which attempts to bring Being under the various categories of knowledge and judgment.[46] Whence – so it is argued – that epochal 'forgetfulness of Being' whose history is coterminous with 'Western metaphysics' and whose stages would include all those later claims to refine or improve upon Aristotle's system, or to provide such knowledge with a transcendental grounding in the manner of Descartes, Kant, or Husserl. However, as I have said, there is another depth-ontological reading of Aristotle that regards him as the first thinker to have espoused a causal-realist approach to the natural sciences and an epistemology that respected the difference – the knowledge-constitutive difference – between our beliefs and whatever it is about the world that makes those beliefs either true or false.[47] On this view much of Aristotle's thinking – including his doctrine of the categories – has had to be revised as a result of later scientific advances, among them (most recently) relativity theory and quantum mechanics. But insofar as metaphysics is 'prior to physics' it is in the sense of providing a more adequate account of those *necessary presuppositions* which explain how it is – through what process of deepening explanatory grasp – that such advances in knowledge come about.[48] And if one thing is clear at every stage in the process it is the impossibility that science and philosophy should ever have embarked upon this path were it not for the various elaborations and refinements carried out upon Aristotle's doctrine of the categories.

Of course there is no denying that Derrida has been deeply influenced by Heidegger and that his reading of Aristotle bears the mark of that influence.[49] All the same, one can trace the clear outlines of a counter-argument in Derrida's work – especially in 'White Mythology' and 'The Supplement of Copula' – which would tend to support that other kind of depth-ontological approach, one that accepts both the necessity of categorical judgement (in more Kantian terms: of bringing intuitions under adequate concepts) and the requirement that such concepts answer to something in the nature of physical reality. I shall now cite some further passages to just this effect, passages having to do with the relationship between concept and metaphor, the role of models or analogies in scientific thought, and that idea of critical 'rectification' which Derrida takes up – albeit in nuanced or qualified form – from the writings of Bachelard and Canguilhem. My point is that these passages presuppose the existence of a real-world, ontologically prior domain in the absence of which there could be no thinking to any purpose about issues in science, epistemology, or philosophy of mind and language. For there are indeed 'good' and 'bad' metaphors as judged from the standpoint of particular disciplines or branches of knowledge. That is to say, some metaphors prove themselves capable of progressive 'rectification' through a process of jointly conceptual and empirical research, a process whose stages are well described in Canguilhem's account of the cellular metaphor in biology or Bachelard's analysis of the way that figures of the circle and the ellipse functioned in astronomical thinking from Aristotle to Newton.[50] What is involved here is undoubtedly a question of propriety, of the extent to which apt, fitting or productive metaphors can be distinguished from others that resist such forms of conceptual elaboration or critique and which thus belong more to the realm of imaginative 'reverie', as Bachelard terms it.[51]

Indeed there may be cases where this process operates in reverse, where a good metaphor 'can work for the critical rectification of a concept, reveal a concept as a bad metaphor, or finally "illustrate" a new concept'.[52] To this extent the metaphor–concept dichotomy is one that requires deconstruction, not only as a result of those complications that can be shown to arise in the various (mostly philosophical) texts devoted to this topic, but also as a matter of explaining how it is that science achieves such conceptual advances. On the other hand metaphors may 'seduce reason' or constitute a kind of 'verbal obstacle' that impedes any progress beyond the first stage of naive, imagistic, or anthropomorphic thinking. Thus, according to Bachelard, 'the danger of immediate metaphors in the formation of the scientific spirit is that they are not always passing images; they push toward an autonomous kind of thought; they tend to completion and fulfilment in the domain of the image'.[53] Again it might be countered that Derrida is not so much propounding this argument as citing Bachelard's use of it in order to mark off his own, more sceptical or anti-realist position. Nor can this rejoinder be lightly dismissed given the many passages in Derrida's work where he makes very conscious and deliberate play with forms of intertextual allusion or variants of the distinction between 'use' and 'mention' invoked by analytic philosophers.[54] Nevertheless I would put the case that the logic of his argument in 'White Mythology' requires that we should understand Derrida (like Bachelard) as accepting the distinction between 'good' and 'bad' metaphors, along with the necessity of applying that distinction to issues in the history and philosophy of science.

This case finds support in his reading of Aristotle, a reading that encompasses Aristotle's treatment of physics, biology, metaphysics, ontology, epistemology, and – not least – the role of metaphor as a heuristic device in these and other fields of enquiry. In Derrida's words: '[t]he ideal of every language, and in particular of metaphor, being to bring to knowledge the thing itself, the turn of speech will be better if it brings us closer to the thing's essential or proper truth' ('White Mythology', p. 238). Again, it would be precipitate to read this passage as a straightforward endorsement, on Derrida's part, of the thesis that language either can or should aim toward the said ideal. But there are, it seems to me, much greater (indeed insuperable) problems with any reading that would treat it purely as *oratio obliqua*, as a statement whose Aristotelian provenance is sufficient to signal its belonging to the realm of a naively realist metaphysics or ontology. For this is to forget what Derrida remarks in his commentary on Bachelard and Canguilhem: that to 'deconstruct' the concept–metaphor distinction is not for one moment to deny that metaphors – 'good' metaphors – can themselves play a formative or decisive role in the production of scientific knowledge. Nor should it be taken as read that when Derrida describes such good metaphors as 'bringing us closer to the thing's essential or proper truth' he must be paraphrasing Aristotle with the purpose of emphatically marking his distance from any such (nowadays discredited) essentialist conception. For in fact that conception has enjoyed an impressive revival in recent philosophical semantics, a development largely owing to work on modal logic by Kripke, Putnam, Evans and Donnellan, among others.[55] This has done much to vindicate the claim that there exists an order of a posteriori necessary truths, that is to say, items of knowledge – such as 'water = H_2O' or 'gold is the metallic element with atomic number 79' – whose standing is contingent on discovery-procedures or the results of empirical enquiry, but whose truth-value is fixed by their reference and therefore holds as a matter of necessity for this and all physically congruent worlds. It has also gone along with a kindred revival of causal-realist theories in present-day philosophy of science, developed very often in response to the perceived shortcomings of logical empiricism.[56]

Again we might recall what Derrida establishes (I think beyond reasonable doubt) in 'The Supplement of Copula': that 'on this matter no analysis will either circumvent or exclude the tribunal of Aristotelianism'. Here it is a question of the categories – the forms or modalities of predicative judgment – and of Aristotle's claim to distinguish a priori between substance and attribute (or essence and accident) by application of those same categories. Thus Derrida puts the case (to recapitulate briefly) that Benveniste cannot be right – that his argument runs into manifest self-contradiction – when he claims to demonstrate the language-relative, the 'contingent' or 'empirical' character of Aristotle's reasoning. But it is equally clear that the doctrine of the categories (along with all its subsequent refinements, elaborations, science-led revisions, and so on) stands or falls with the realist argument for regarding them *not* as mere conceptual schemes devoid of determinate reference, but rather as providing veridical knowledge of that to which they properly apply. For otherwise Benveniste could simply point out – with ample support from the recent philosophical literature – that 'conceptual scheme' is just a place-filling substitute for 'language', and that his charge against Aristotle (of purporting to 'reason in the absolute' while in fact reasoning in terms supplied by the Greek language) still holds good no matter which of these alternative idioms one chooses to deploy.

In short, Derrida's entire argument would collapse – here as in 'White Mythology' – were it taken to exclude those components of Aristotle's theory that link the categorical nature of judgment to the nature of a 'thing's essential or proper truth'. And this applies also to 'good' metaphors, principally those which Aristotle defines as belonging to the fourth type, the kind whose meaning is best explained by the double-analogy or proportion-scheme model. Their particular virtue, as Aristotle sees it, is to 'bring us knowledge of something new' through a complex transfer of significations from things already known or terms that possess some familiar range of reference. Thus (from Book III of the *Rhetoric*): '[m]etaphors must be drawn ... from things that are related to the original thing, and yet not obviously so related – just as in philosophy also an acute mind will perceive resemblances even in things far apart'.[57] But such knowledge will count for nothing, in Aristotle's view, if it is a knowledge only of nominal definitions or of the meanings that attach to this or that term by virtue of linguistic convention.

Derrida's immense respect for Aristotle is evident in many of his writings, most often when he shows how later philosophers – Hegel and Heidegger among them – have thought to go 'beyond' some limitation or unresolved issue in Aristotle's thought, only to produce another (less perspicuous) rehearsal of the same dilemma.[58] Such (as we have seen) is his argument in the essay on Benveniste, where Aristotle's doctrine of the categories is taken as possessing absolute (transcategorial) validity with respect to any thesis concerning the order of relationship between thought and language. With 'White Mythology' the case is more complex – or Derrida's attitude more ambivalent – since here the argument comes into tension with a Nietzsche-derived emphasis on the ubiquity of metaphor in the texts of philosophy which exerts a strong countervailing influence. This tension is perhaps most obvious in a passage where Derrida asks us to imagine what might be involved – or what conditions would need to be satisfied – in any project that attempted 'a simultaneously historic and systematic sampling of philosophical metaphors'. First, he writes,

> it would have to be governed by a rigorous concept of metaphor, a concept to be carefully distinguished, within a general tropology, from all the other turns of speech with which metaphor is too often confused. Provisionally, let us take such a definition for granted. One would then have to acknowledge the importation into so-called philosophical discourse of exogenous metaphors, or rather of significations that become metaphorical in being transported out of their own habitat. Thus, one would classify the places they come from: there would be metaphors that are biological, organic, mechanical, technical, economic, historical, mathematical – geometric, topologic, arithmetical – (supposing that in the strict sense there might be mathematical metaphors, a problem to be held in reserve for now). This classification, which supposes an indigenous population and a migration, is usually adopted by those, not numerous, who have studied the metaphorics of a single philosopher or a particular body of work. ('White Mythology', p. 220)

Of the many points that could made about this passage let me offer the following as most relevant here. (1) Whatever his Nietzschean reservations with respect to that idea of 'a rigorous concept of metaphor' Derrida has striven to articulate just such a concept throughout 'White Mythology'. (2) It is only on this basis that one can make adequate sense of Derrida's requirement that metaphor ('good' or well-defined metaphor) be distinguished from those other less rigorously specified 'turns of speech' with which it is all too often confused. (3) Any attempted 'classification' of the various types of metaphor – biological, organic, mechanical, and so on – will need to take account of the various knowledge-constitutive domains to which those metaphors properly apply. (4) One could list Bachelard, Canguilhem, and Derrida himself among those thinkers ('not very numerous') who have in fact carried this analysis into various particular 'bodies of thought'. (5) The result, in Derrida's case, is to show that any over-generalized or indiscriminate notion of metaphor is incapable of explaining the fitness criteria – the standards of truth and falsehood – that ultimately distinguish 'good' from 'bad' metaphors in this or that specific region of enquiry. And (6), those regions are themselves to be distinguished in virtue of the defining properties – the constitutive features, causal mechanisms, real as distinct from nominal attributes – which constitute their appropriate object-domain. For (7), it is impossible that metaphors should yield knowledge except through the kinds of complex analogy that involve both categorical (predicative) judgments and the ability to 'perceive resemblances' on the basis of a genuine – *de re* and not merely *de dicto* – affinity between terms in the implied structure of comparison.

As I say, there are many indications in 'White Mythology' that Derrida would resist such a reading of his argument, or at any rate direct us to those other passages where it is affirmed (categorically) that no theory of metaphor can ever be fully adequate to the task of conceptual exegesis and categorization. Still I should venture that this reading is called for as a matter of conceptual necessity if that argument is to be treated at anything like its own high level of sustained analytical grasp. After all, Derrida would be the last to require that we should read so slavishly or uncritically as to take his every utterance on trust. His critique of Benveniste is a much better model here, along with those other essays – on Plato, Aristotle, Kant, Husserl, Levinas, or J.L. Austin – where Derrida is true to his own principle (stated most succinctly in a well-known passage from *Of Grammatology*): that while a deconstructive reading cannot dispense with the strictest protocols of fidelity to the text in hand, it is none the less at some point bound to raise issues that go beyond this most elementary of requirements.[59] And in his dealing with the question of metaphor it seems to me that there is a whole dimension of Derrida's thought which presupposes a critical-realist ontology at odds with some of his more sceptical (or overtly Nietzschean) pronouncements.

I shall instance one last passage from 'White Mythology' where this question is posed with oblique but unmistakable force.

> If we went back to each term in the definition proposed by the *Poetics*, we could recognise in it the mark of a figure (*metaphora* or *epiphora* is also a movement of spatial translation; *eidos* is also a visible figure, a contour and a form, the space of an aspect of a species; *genos* is also an affiliation, the base of a birth, of an origin, of a family, and so on). All that these tropes maintain and sediment in the entangling of their roots is apparent. However, the issue is not to take the function of the concept back to the etymology of the noun along a straight line. We have been attentive to the internal, systematic, and synchronic articulation of the Aristotelian concepts in order to avoid this etymologism. Nevertheless, none of their names being a

> conventional and arbitrary *X*, the historical or genealogical (let us not say etymological) tie of the signified concept to its signifier (to language) is not contingent. (pp. 252–3)

First we should note the caution against naive 'etymologism', against the fallacy – as Derrida thinks it – of tracing 'the concept back to the etymology of the noun' along a path whose (surely Heideggerian) end-point is the appeal to some primordial truth-content obscured by the subsequent history of 'metaphysical' or technologico-scientific accretions. To think in these terms is to ignore the possibility that metaphors may acquire cognitive or epistemological yield in virtue of their appropriateness to the topic in hand and their capacity for critical 'rectification' through the process described by Bachelard and Canguilhem. It is also – I would argue – to open the way for all manner of irrationalist pseudo-profundities and a resultantly confused idea of the relation between science, epistemology, and ethical issues. Derrida would never go so far in his criticism of Heidegger. But the above passage does at least suggest how thinking can be led astray through an over-reliance on etymologies (genuine or false) that supposedly give access to a truth beyond reach of analysis or conceptual understanding.

It is in order to avoid such confusion, Derrida writes, that his essay has been duly attentive to 'the internal, systematic, and synchronic articulation of the Aristotelian concepts'. By so doing it prevents any premature recourse to a generalized notion of metaphor, one that would give no hold for the sorts of distinction that Aristotle draws between simple and complex, vague and precise, or routine and innovatory (that is, heuristically productive) examples of the kind. Still one may doubt whether this structural-synchronic approach – derived from the working methodology of Saussurean linguistics – is in itself fully adequate to explain the fact that some metaphors (like those of the cellular structure of living tissue, the 'circulation' of blood, or the ellipse as a figure for planetary motion) have attained the status of scientific concepts and thus proved amenable to further elaboration, criticism, and investigative research.[60] For it is among the most basic axioms of structural linguistics – and likewise of any method in the human or the natural sciences which takes its bearings from that pilot discipline – that language is pre-eminently a system of relationships and differences 'without positive terms'.[61] Thus in order for linguistics to become a genuine science it must bracket or suspend any concern with the referent (the putative object of discourse) and focus instead on those two dimensions of language – the orders of the signifier and the signified – where meaning is solely and exclusively a product of the differential interplay or network of contrastive relations that constitute the proper (theoretically specified) object of any such linguistic science.[62] No doubt there is a sense – an everyday, practical sense – in which speakers manage to refer to certain objects, states of affairs, items of shared perceptual or conceptual acquaintance, and so forth. But from the strictly linguistic (structural-synchronic) standpoint such observations are beside the point. For only by excluding any extra-linguistic ground of appeal can this discipline achieve the status of a mature science, one whose theoretical apparatus is nowhere compromised by a dependence on assumptions drawn from outside its own disciplinary domain.

This is not the place for a detailed account of the various problems that structuralism encountered in its attempt to extend Saussure's model to other regions of enquiry. Sufficient to say that it has often produced an outlook of *de rigueur* epistemological scepticism whose damaging results across a range of disciplines from historiography to political theory and 'science studies' are still very much with us.[63] (In justice to Saussure it should perhaps be pointed out that this whole later chapter of developments went far beyond anything explicitly projected in the *Course in General Linguistics*.) However, my main concern here is with Derrida's invocation of this model as a means of bringing adequate rigour to the discussion of metaphor as a philosophic topos and – more specifically – as a means of conceptual advance in the natural and human sciences. Consider his statement, with reference to Aristotle, that 'none of their names being a conventional and arbitrary X, the historical and genealogical (let us not say etymological) tie of the signified concept to its signifier (to language) is not contingent' ('White Mythology', p. 253). That the argument is distinctly under strain at this point is suggested by the tortuous grammar, the multiplied negatives, and the somewhat wiredrawn terminological distinctions. For Derrida is not only implying a criticism of Heidegger – elsewhere such a powerful presence in 'White Mythology' – as having fallen prey to a species of naive 'etymologism' that confuses the issue with regard to metaphor.[64] He is also rejecting any version of the linguistic-conventionalist thesis which would have it that 'names' attach to 'concepts' only through an 'arbitrary' order of relationship, one which is therefore purely 'contingent' upon the way that language happens to distribute its twofold economy of signifiers and signifieds. For when Aristotle sets out to define metaphor it is not just a matter of some 'conventional and arbitrary X' – some particular one among a range of possible signifiers – which occupies that role. Rather it is the case that Aristotle's chosen terms of analysis (his language of genus and species, of resemblance, analogy, proportion-schemes and so forth) are terms peculiarly fitted to the purpose in virtue of their proven descriptive, conceptual, and explanatory yield.

This is why Derrida can argue – despite his own just-previous appeal to a conventionalist or structural-synchronic paradigm – that 'the tie of the signified concept to its signifier (to language) is not contingent'. On the contrary: it is a given and *necessary* tie insofar as certain terms are definitionally equivalent to certain operative concepts, and insofar as those concepts have their rightful application (their determinate validity-conditions) in certain specific areas of enquiry. Thus Aristotle's four chief types of metaphor – together with the (no doubt metaphoric) terms that Aristotle uses to define them – cannot be viewed as so many 'arbitrary' constructs out of a language, the ancient Greek, whose conceptual resources were 'contingent' on its lexico-grammatical structure, and which hence merely chanced to throw up those particular quasi-universal definitions. It is just this kind of relativizing argument that Derrida finds strictly unintelligible when Benveniste applies it to Aristotle's doctrine of the categories. And the same difficulty arises with metaphor since here also the proffered definitions are *categorical* insofar as they have to do with judgments – of space, form, 'visible figure', resemblance, analogy, species- or genus-inclusion, and so on – without which there could be no purposeful thinking about any topic whatsoever.

Such is the transcendental argument in its weak (highly generalized but essentially negative) 'condition of impossibility' form. 'Weak', that is to say, in the sense that it goes no further than theorists like Davidson toward offering an adequate (substantive) set of truth-conditions or validity-criteria applicable to metaphoric discourse.[65] What is further required is a realist ontology of the kind that Derrida nowhere explicitly endorses, but which none the less figures as a necessary presupposition if his arguments are to hold good. To this extent one is justified, I think, in reading 'White Mythology' as Derrida reads Benveniste in 'The Supplement of Copula'. That is to say, where Derrida establishes (*contra* Benveniste) the 'rigorous and principled impossibility' of relativizing Aristotle's categories to language in the manner proposed, so again it can be shown (*contra* Derrida) that this argument would lack demonstrative force were it not that some such categories possess a real-world ontological grounding. Hence the fact that certain metaphors – those which involve the analogical transfer of attributes from one category or kind of object to another – are able to provide genuine knowledge or even (on occasion) a decisive advance in scientific understanding. Such, I take it, is the chief lesson to be learned from those studies in the history and philosophy of science that stress the role of metaphor as a heuristic device subject to critical evaluation in terms of its cognitive or epistemological yield.[66] Whatever his express reservations in this regard – his reading of Bachelard and Canguilhem very largely through the lens of a structural-synchronic analysis of language joined to a sceptical (Nietzschean) 'genealogy' of truth-related concepts and values – Derrida none the less makes it clear that such concepts and values are strictly indissociable from the project of epistemo-critical thought. What is indeed so impressive about 'White Mythology' is this readiness to place its own more programmatical claims in question through a rigorous process of immanent critique that holds those claims to scientific and philosophical account.

Only thus – it seems to me – can we make adequate sense of his statement with regard to Aristotle's paradigm instances of metaphor: namely, that 'none of their names being a conventional or arbitrary X, the ... tie of the signified concept to its signifier (to language) is not contingent' (p. 253). This may perchance remind us of some of Davidson's more casual or throwaway assertions, such as his claim (from 'A Nice Derangement of Epitaphs') that there is 'no such thing as a language', or – from 'The Very Idea of a Conceptual Scheme' – that 'in giving up the dualism of scheme and world we do not give up the world, but re-establish unmediated touch with the familiar objects whose antics make our sentences true or false'.[67] However, they arrive at these conclusions by very different routes and with a very different sense of what it means to give up thinking in linguistic-conventionalist terms. Davidson's is a kind of flat, no-nonsense empiricism which rejects the dichotomy of 'scheme and world' – along with all its consequent problems – but can offer nothing in its place bar the vague appeal to 'passing theories' as an *ad hoc* (scarcely adequate) solution. Derrida's approach, conversely, is one that goes a long and complicated way around and which – true to its Saussurean lights – eschews any overt talk of the extra-linguistic referent in favour of a dualist (signifier–signified) model of discursive representation. And yet, despite this, 'White Mythology' offers a far more cogent analysis of metaphor, of its role in scientific, philosophical and other sorts of discourse, than anything available from Davidson's minimalist account. For when Derrida concludes that the tie between signifier and signified cannot be thought of as 'arbitrary', 'conventional', or 'contingent' this is not just a matter – as with Davidson – of adopting that crypto-pragmatist line of least resistance which equates meaning and truth with whatever works best for our current interpretive purposes. Rather it is a position that his essay has achieved through a detailed and meticulous treatment of issues in ontology, epistemology, metaphysics, linguistics, and the history and philosophy of science. What this analysis reveals – among other things – is the fact that such a project cannot elude the critical 'tribunal' of Aristotelian thought, whether as concerns the categorical nature of thinking and judgment in general, or as concerns its necessary grounding in a real-world (mind- and language-independent) ontical domain.

Metaphor, Mimesis, and the Growth of Knowledge

'Meaning and reference', Derrida writes: 'that is, the possibility of signifying by means of a noun'. And, continuing in this Aristotelian mode:

> What is proper to nouns is to signify something, an independent being identical to itself, conceived as such. It is at this point that the theory of the name, such as it is implied by the concept of metaphor, is articulated with ontology ... The definition of metaphor is in its place in the *Poetics*, which opens as a treatise on *mimesis*. *Mimesis* is never without the theoretical perception of resemblance or similarity, that is, of that which will always be posited as the condition for metaphor. *Homoiosis* ['adequation' or 'correspondence'] is not only constitutive of the value of truth (*aletheia*) which governs the entire chain; it is that without which the metaphorical operation is impossible ... The condition for metaphor (for good and true metaphor) is the condition for truth ... *Mimesis* thus determined belongs to *logos* ... it is tied to the possibility of meaning and truth in discourse ... Metaphor, thus, as an effect of *mimesis* and *homoiosis*, the manifestation of analogy, will be a means of knowledge, a means that is subordinate, but certain. ('White Mythology', pp. 237–8)

We are now better placed to assess the status – the 'enunciative modality', as post-structuralists would phrase it, but also the constative or assertoric status – of passages like this where Derrida is in some sense rehearsing Aristotle's arguments. I hope to have shown that they cannot be regarded as *mere* rehearsals, offered up (so to speak) as handy material for knock-down deconstructive treatment on the familiar (quasi-Derridean) lines: 'all concepts are metaphors', 'all truth-claims rhetorical', 'all philosophy a species of poetry or fiction', and so on. Such is no doubt the most tempting construal for literary theorists keen to exploit any chance of reversing the received (philosophical) order of priority between truth-related terms – *logos*, *homoiosis*, *aletheia* – and those, like mimesis, that philosophers since Plato have often treated as belonging to an inferior realm of fictive or poetic representation. But this approach simply won't work for 'White Mythology', unless by excising whole portions of Derrida's argument and reading what remains with a scant regard for its precise articulations of detail.

To be sure it may be said that the above passage evokes (via Aristotle) a systematic linkage between, on the one hand, truth and its various associated values and, on the other, a concept like mimesis whose primary application is to poetry, drama, and the visual arts. However, this gives no warrant for the idea that Derrida has 'deconstructed' those values to the point where they figure as purely rhetorical or fictive constructs. For it is exactly Derrida's point that mimesis for Aristotle has a truth-content – a relationship (through metaphor) to *logos* and *homoiosis* –

whereby it assumes an essential and productive role in the process of human knowledge-acquisition. Such was of course the chief ground of Aristotle's quarrel with Plato over the value of mimetic representation in the verbal and visual domains. For Plato this could only be a source of error and illusion, a making-do with false appearances that were twice removed from ultimate reality. Thus the artist imitated those objects of sensuous (phenomenal) cognition which were themselves mere copies of 'forms' or 'ideas' that belonged to a realm beyond the reach of quotidian experience.[68] When the carpenter constructed a table he was at least applying his artisanal skills – his practical or workaday knowledge – to the production of an object with genuine use-value, albeit one whose 'true' nature (whose participation in the form 'table') was such as could only be grasped by an intellect capable of rising above such mundane concerns. But when the artist set out to 'imitate' a table – to portray it in painting or describe it in words – he possessed neither the carpenter's skill in matters of craft and design nor the philosopher's wisdom to seek true knowledge in that higher (suprasensible) realm. Like the Sophists or rhetoricians his only skill was in offering a mere semblance of knowledge, a claim to all-purpose expertise – in the arts, sciences, history, politics, military matters, and so forth – which enabled him to deceive those credulous types who failed to see beyond appearances.

All this is of course familiar enough from standard scholarly and philosophical accounts of what Plato was already describing as the 'ancient quarrel' between philosophy and poetry. It is also well-known that Aristotle defended the claims of poetic mimesis against Plato's charge by linking it to the most basic of human cognitive powers, the capacity for acquiring knowledge through those various forms of imitation – perceptual, behavioral, linguistic, practical, ethico-political, and so on – all of which had a vital part to play in the process of educative character-formation.[69] Thus he rejected Plato's other-worldly idealist ontology in favour of a strongly empirical commitment to knowledge as the product of human interaction with those real-world objects, processes, and events whose nature could best be understood through the methods of the physical sciences and not through the contemplation of abstract Forms or Essences. Hence Aristotle's very different view of mimesis, metaphor and rhetoric, each taken as a valid means of advancing or communicating knowledge just so long as their truth-claims were carefully distinguished from those of the more rigorous sciences or modes of inductive reasoning. Even so these latter could scarcely have developed – or continued to make progress – were it not for the role of mimesis and metaphor in opening up new and productive regions of enquiry. For it is precisely the virtue of 'good' metaphors to provide a basis for analogical reasoning from things already known to things whose properties can best be inferred through the perception of resemblance or natural-kind affinity. In other words there is always a mimetic component in the process of knowledge-acquisition, whatever those subsequent stages of advance that enable thinking to reduce its dependence on 'naive' or 'unrectified' images, metaphors, and modes of perceptual-intuitive grasp.

This is why Aristotle can turn the tables on Plato in a passage from Book III of the *Metaphysics* (cited by Derrida) where it is very much a question of 'good' versus 'bad' or truthful as opposed to specious uses of metaphor. Thus 'Aristotle reproaches Plato for being satisfied with "poetic" metaphors (*metaphoras legein poietikas*) and for keeping to hollow language (*kenologein*) when he says that Ideas are the paradigms within which other things participate' ('White Mythology', p. 238). It is not that such 'poetic' figures are inherently false, misleading, or deceptive; rather that Plato – himself elsewhere such a stern opponent of metaphor – has here fallen prey to the kind of ontological confusion which results from taking those metaphors at face value and erecting an entire metaphysics upon them.[70] Aristotle's criticism marks him out very clearly as a precursor of those recent movements in philosophy of language and science which still represent the most developed alternative to idealist, conventionalist, or anti-realist views. Roy Bhaskar makes the point with admirable succinctness when he asks which constitutes the better explanation of the colour blue: the idea that blue objects are those which 'participate' in the Form or the Essence of blueness, or the fact that their surfaces are such as to absorb or reflect light-waves within a certain (experimentally determined) frequency-range.[71] Of course there is a sense in which this latter explanation might itself be described as 'metaphorical', relying as it does on a wave-theory of light which happens to work very well in this context – hence its intuitive appeal – but which would need to be 'rectified' in view of more advanced (quantum-mechanical or wave–particle dualist) accounts. But this does nothing to diminish the force of Aristotle's argument against Plato, any more than the fact that he (Aristotle) possessed not an inkling of these present-day scientific theories. For what makes his approach altogether more adequate in scientific or causal-explanatory terms is its openness to just such forms of progressive development, elaboration, and critique.

University of Wales, Cardiff

Notes

[1] Jacques Derrida, 'The Supplement of Copula', in *Margins of Philosophy*, trans. Alan Bass (Chicago: University of Chicago Press, 1982), pp. 175–205.

[2] See especially Richard Rorty, 'Philosophy as a Kind of Writing: an essay on Derrida', in *Consequences of Pragmatism* (Brighton: Harvester, 1982), pp. 90–109; 'Deconstruction and Circumvention', in *Essays on Heidegger and Others* (Cambridge: Cambridge University Press, 1991), pp. 85–106. See also Christopher Norris, 'Philosophy as *Not* Just a "Kind of Writing": Derrida and the claim of reason', in R.W. Dasenbrock (ed.), *Redrawing the Lines: analytic philosophy, deconstruction, and literary theory* (Minneapolis: University of Minnesota Press, 1989), pp. 189–203; Rorty, 'Two Meanings of "Logocentrism": a reply to Norris', ibid., pp. 204–16.

[3] See for instance Derrida, 'Afterword: toward an ethic of discussion', in *Limited Inc* (2nd edn, ed. Gerald Graff, Evanston, Ill.: Northwestern University Press, 1989); also 'Letter to a Japanese Friend', trans. David Wood and Andrew Benjamin, in David Wood and Robert Bernasconi (eds), *Derrida and Différance* (Northwestern University Press, 1988), pp. 1–5; 'Deconstruction in America' (interview), *Critical Exchange*, No. 17 (Winter 1985), pp. 1–32.

[4] Rorty, 'Philosophy as a Kind of Writing' (op. cit.).

[5] Stephen Schiffer, *Remnants of Meaning* (Cambridge, Mass.: M.I.T. Press, 1987); see also Steven Stich, *The Fragmentation of Reason* (M.I.T. Press, 1990).

[6] Donald Davidson, *Inquiries into Truth and Interpretation* (Oxford: Clarendon Press, 1984); 'A Nice Derangement of Epitaphs', in Ernest Lepore (ed.), *Truth and Interpretation: perspectives on the work of Donald Davidson* (Oxford: Blackwell, 1986), pp. 433–46.

[7] See Rorty, *Consequences of Pragmatism* (op. cit.); also *Contingency, Irony, and Solidarity* (Cambridge: Cambridge University Press, 1989); *Objectivity, Relativism, and Truth* (Cambridge University Press, 1991) and *Essays on Heidegger and Others* (Cambridge University Press, 1991).

[8] See for instance Shekhar Pradhan, 'Minimalist Semantics: Davidson and Derrida on meaning, use, and convention', *Diacritics*, Vol. 16, No. 1 (1986), pp. 66–77; Samuel C. Wheeler, 'Indeterminacy of French Translation: Derrida and Davidson', in Lepore, *Truth and Interpretation* (op. cit.), pp. 477–94.

[9] Derrida, *Limited Inc* (op. cit.).

[10] Derrida, 'The Supplement of Copula' (op. cit.): all further references given by title and page-number in the text. See also Emile Benveniste, *Problems In General Linguistics*, trans. Mary E. Meek (Coral Gables: University of Miami Press, 1971).

[11] The passages of Aristotle here referred to are to be found in the *Categories*, Chapter 4 and *Metaphysics*, Chapter 6.

[12] Benveniste, *Problems* (op. cit.), p. 57.

[13] Ibid., p. 56.

[14] Ibid., p. 61.

[15] Schiffer, *Remnants of Meaning* (op. cit.); see also Rorty, *Consequences of Pragmatism* and other citations in note 7, above.

[16] On this aspect of Derrida's work see especially Rodolphe Gasché, *The Tain of the Mirror: Derrida and the philosophy of reflection* (Cambridge, Mass.: Harvard University Press, 1986).

[17] W.V. Quine, 'Two Dogmas of Empiricism', in *From a Logical Point of View* (Cambridge, Mass.: Harvard University Press, 1961), pp. 20–46; *Ontological Relativity and Other Essays* (New York: Columbia University Press, 1969); also Davidson, *Inquiries into Truth and Interpretation* (op. cit.); David C. Hoy, *The Critical Circle: literature, history, and philosophical hermeneutics* (Berkeley & Los Angeles: University of California Press, 1978); J.E. Malpas, *Donald Davidson and the Mirror of Meaning* (Cambridge: Cambridge University Press, 1992); Mark Okrent, *Heidegger's Pragmatism: understanding, being, and the critique of metaphysics* (Ithaca, N.Y.: Cornell University Press, 1988); Hilary Putnam, 'Meaning Holism', in L.E. Hahn and P.A. Schilpp (eds), *The Philosophy of W.V. Quine* (La Salle, Ill.: Open Court, 1986), pp. 405–26; Rorty, *Philosophy and the Mirror of Nature* (Oxford: Blackwell, 1980); Stich, *The Fragmentation of Reason* (op. cit.); Wheeler, 'Indeterminacy of French Translation' (op. cit.). For a critical survey of these and related arguments, see Jerry Fodor and Ernest Lepore, *Holism: a shopper's guide* (Oxford: Blackwell, 1991).

[18] See Pradhan, 'Minimalist Semantics', and Wheeler, 'Indeterminacy of French Translation' (cited in note 8, above); also my criticism of their arguments in Norris, 'Reading Donald Davidson: truth, meaning and right interpretation', *Deconstruction and the Interests of Theory* (London: Pinter, 1988), pp. 59–83.

[19] Derrida, *'Speech and Phenomena' and Other Essays on Husserl's Theory of Signs*, trans. David B. Allison (Evanston, Ill.: Northwestern University Press, 1972); see also *Margins of Philosophy* (op. cit.) and *Writing and Difference*, trans. Alan Bass (London: Routledge & Kegan Paul, 1978).

[20] See Rorty, *Philosophy and the Mirror of Nature* (op. cit.).

[21] See especially Derrida, *Margins of Philosophy* (op. cit.).

[22] Derrida, 'White Mythology: metaphor in the text of philosophy', in *Margins of Philosophy* (op. cit.), pp. 207–71.

[23] Rorty, 'Science as Solidarity', 'Is Natural Science a Natural Kind?', and 'Texts and Lumps', in *Objectivity, Relativism, and Truth* (op. cit.), pp. 35–45, 46–62 and 78–92.

[24] See for instance Roy Bhaskar, *Scientific Realism and Human Emancipation* (London: Verso, 1986); *Reclaiming Reality: a critical introduction to contemporary philosophy* (Verso, 1989).
[25] Cited in note 3, above.
[26] Nietzsche, 'On Truth and Falsity in their Ultramoral Sense', in Oscar Levy (ed.), *The Complete Works of Friedrich Nietzsche*, Vol. 2 (New York: Russell & Russell, 1964).
[27] See Maudemarie Clark, *Nietzsche on Truth and Philosophy* (Cambridge: Cambridge University Press, 1990); also Malcolm Pasley (ed.), *Nietzsche: imagery and thought* (London: Routledge & Kegan Paul, 1978) and – from a Heideggerian/postmodernist standpoint – Babette E. Babich, *Nietzsche's Philosophy of Science: reflecting science on the ground of art and life* (Albany, N.Y.: State University of New York Press, 1994).
[28] See for instance Georges Canguilhem, *La connaissance de la vie* (Paris: Vrin, 1969); *Etudes d'histoire et de philosophie des sciences* (Vrin, 1968); Gaston Bachelard, *The Philosophy of No: a philosophy of the new scientific mind* (New York: Orion Press, 1968); *La formation de l'esprit scientifique* (Paris: Corti, 1938); *The New Scientific Spirit* (Boston: Beacon Press, 1984); also Mary Tiles, *Bachelard: science and objectivity* (Cambridge: Cambridge University Press, 1984) and Dominique Lecourt, *Marxism and Epistemology: Bachelard, Canguilhem and Foucault* (London: New Left Books, 1975).
[29] Canguilhem, *La connaissance de la vie* (op. cit.), pp. 64–5; cited by Derrida, 'White Mythology', p. 263.
[30] Derrida, 'White Mythology', p. 264.
[31] For a fairly representative sampling see Hilary Lawson and Lisa Appignanesi (eds), *Dismantling Truth: reality in the postmodern world* (London: Weidenfeld & Nicolson, 1989).
[32] Bertrand Russell, *The Problems of Philosophy* (London: Oxford University Press, 1912), p. 130. See also Russell, *On the Philosophy of Science* (Indianapolis: Bobbs-Merrill, 1965).
[33] See for instance Barry Barnes, *About Science* (Oxford: Blackwell, 1985); Steve Fuller, *Philosophy of Science and its Discontents* (Boulder, Colorado: Westview Press, 1988); K. Knorr-Cetina and M. Mulkay (eds), *Science Observed* (London: Sage, 1983); Derek L. Phillips, *Wittgenstein and Scientific Knowledge: a sociological perspective* (London: Macmillan, 1977); Richard Rorty, *Objectivity, Relativism, and Truth* (op. cit.); Joseph Rouse, *Knowledge and Power: toward a political philosophy of science* (Ithaca, N.Y.: Cornell University Press, 1987); Steve Woolgar, *Science: the very idea* (London: Tavistock, 1988).
[34] Benveniste, *Problems in General Linguistics* (op. cit.), p. 57.
[35] Ibid., p. 55.
[36] See Ferdinand de Saussure, *Course in General Linguistics*, trans. Wade Baskin (London: Fontana, 1974).
[37] Derrida, '"Genesis and Structure" and Phenomenology', in *Writing and Difference* (op. cit.), pp. 154–68; p. 159.
[38] Aristotle, *Poetics*, trans. I. Bayswater, in W.D. Ross (ed.), *The Works of Aristotle* (London: Oxford University Press, 1924), 1457b6–9).
[39] See for instance J. Hillis Miller, 'Remembering and Disremembering in Nietzsche's "On Truth and Lies in a Non-Moral Sense"', *Boundary* 2, Vol. 9 (1981), pp. 41–54.
[40] See Gasché, *The Tain of the Mirror* (op. cit.) for a detailed and authoritative treatment.
[41] See for instance John R. Searle, 'Reiterating the Differences', *Glyph*, Vol. 1 (1977), pp. 198–208; also – at a far higher level of philosophic grasp – J. Claude Evans, *Strategies of Deconstruction: Derrida and the myth of the voice* (Minneapolis: University of Minnesota Press, 1991).

[42] Immanuel Kant, *Critique of Pure Reason*, trans. N. Kemp Smith (London: Macmillan, 1965), p. 113–4.
[43] See note 19, above.
[44] See especially Nietzsche, *Philosophy and Truth: selections from Nietzsche's notebooks of the early 1870s*, trans. and ed. Daniel Breazeale (Atlantic Highlands, N.J.: Humanities Press, 1979); *Friedrich Nietzsche on Rhetoric and Language*, trans. and ed. Sander L. Gilman, Carole Blair, and David J. Parent (London: Oxford University Press, 1989).
[45] Aristotle, *Metaphysics*, trans. Hugh Tredenick (Cambridge, Mass.: Harvard University Press, 1933), p. 299. (Cited in Derrida, 'White Mythology' [op. cit.], p. 183).
[46] Martin Heidegger, *Being and Time*, trans. John Macquarrie and Edward Robinson (Oxford: Blackwell, 1962).
[47] See for instance Rom Harré's excellent brief account of Aristotle as natural scientist in his book *Great Scientific Experiments* (London: Oxford University Press, 1983).
[48] See Imre Lakatos and Alan Musgrave (eds), *Criticism and the Growth of Knowledge* (Cambridge: Cambridge University Press, 1970); Nicholas Rescher, *Scientific Progress* (Oxford: Blackwell, 1979); Rescher, *Scientific Realism: a critical reappraisal* (Dordrecht: D. Reidel, 1987); Wesley C. Salmon, *Scientific Explanation and the Causal Structure of the World* (Princeton, N.J.: Princeton University Press, 1984); Peter J. Smith, *Realism and the Progress of Science* (Cambridge University Press, 1981); John Michael Zimon, *Reliable Knowledge: an exploration of the grounds for belief in science* (Cambridge University Press, 1978).
[49] See Derrida, 'Ousia and Gramme: note on a note from *Being and Time*', in *Margins of Philosophy* (op. cit.), pp. 29–67 for some further examples of the way that Derrida uses Aristotle to reveal certain blindspots, aporias, or non-sequiturs in Heidegger's thinking. See also Herman Rapaport, *Heidegger and Derrida: reflections on time and language* (Lincoln, Nebr.: University of Nebraska Press, 1989).
[50] See Canguilhem, *La connaissance de la vie* and Bachelard, *La formation de l'esprit scientifique* (note 28, above); also – on this topic more generally – Max Black, *Models and Metaphors* (Ithaca, N.Y.: Cornell University Press, 1962); Eva Feder Kitay, *Metaphor: its cognitive force and linguistic structure* (Oxford: Clarendon Press, 1987); W.H. Leatherdale, *The Role of Analogy, Model and Metaphor in Science* (Amsterdam: North-Holland, 1974).
[51] See Bachelard, *The Poetics of Reverie*, trans. Daniel Russell (Boston: Beacon Press, 1971).
[52] Derrida, 'White Mythology' (op. cit.), p. 259.
[53] Bachelard, *La formation de l'esprit scientifique* (op. cit.), p. 81.
[54] See for instance Derrida, 'Signature Event Context' (op. cit.); also 'Envois', in *The Postcard: from Socrates to Freud and beyond*, trans. Alan Bass (Chicago: University of Chicago Press, 1987), pp. 1–256 *passim*.
[55] See Saul Kripke, *Naming and Necessity* (Oxford: Blackwell, 1980); Stephen Schwartz (ed.), *Naming, Necessity, and Natural Kinds* (Ithaca, N.Y.: Cornell University Press, 1977); Gareth Evans, *The Varieties of Reference*, ed. John McDowell (Oxford: Clarendon Press, 1982); M.R. Ayers, 'Locke versus Aristotle on Natural Kinds', *Journal of Philosophy*, Vol. 77 (1981), pp. 247–72; David Wiggins, *Sameness and Substance* (Oxford: Blackwell, 1980).
[56] See for instance Wesley Salmon, *Scientific Explanation and the Causal Structure of the World* (op. cit.); also Salmon, *Four Decades of Scientific Explanation* (Minneapolis: University of Minnesota Press, 1989); D.M. Armstrong, *What Is a Law of Nature?* (Cambridge: Cambridge University Press, 1983); Roy Bhaskar, *Scientific Realism and Human Emancipation* (op. cit.); Rom Harré and E.H. Madden, *Causal Powers* (Oxford: Blackwell, 1975); M. Tooley, *Causation: a realist approach* (Oxford: Blackwell, 1988).
[57] Aristotle, *Rhetoric* III, ii, 1412a9–12; cited by Derrida, 'White Mythology', p. 238n.

⁵⁸ See for instance Derrida, 'Ousia and Gramme' (op. cit.).
⁵⁹ See Derrida, *Of Grammatology*, trans. Gagatri C. Spivak (Baltimore: Johns Hopkins University Press, 1974), p. 158.
⁶⁰ See references to Canguilhem and Bachelard, note 28, above.
⁶¹ Saussure, *Course in General Linguistics* (op. cit.).
⁶² See especially Roy Harris, *Reading Saussure* (London: Duckworth, 1987).
⁶³ For criticism of this overly generalized use of Saussure's linguistic model, see for instance Perry Anderson, *In the Tracks of Historical Materialism* (London: Verso, 1983); Valentine Cunningham, *In the Reading Gaol: postmodernity, texts and history* (Oxford: Blackwell, 1994); Terry Eagleton, *Ideology: an introduction* (London: Verso, 1991); Thomas Pavel, *The Feud of Language: a history of structuralist thought* (Oxford: Blackwell, 1990); Raymond Tallis, *Not Saussure* (London: Macmillan, 1988).
⁶⁴ See also Derrida, 'The Retrait of Metaphor', *Enclitic*, Vol. 2, No. 2 (1978), pp. 5–34
⁶⁵ Donald Davidson, 'What Metaphors Mean', in *Inquiries into Truth and Interpretation* (op. cit.), pp. 245–64.
⁶⁶ See note 50, above.
⁶⁷ Donald Davidson, 'A Nice Derangement of Epitaphs' (note 6, above), p. 446 and 'On the Very Idea of a Conceptual Scheme', in *Inquiries into Truth and Interpretation* (op. cit.), pp. 183–98; p. 198.
⁶⁸ Plato, *The Republic*, ed. James Adam (2 vols., Cambridge: Cambridge University Press, 1902).
⁶⁹ Aristotle, *The Poetics* (op. cit.).
⁷⁰ See also Derrida, 'Plato's Pharmacy', in *Dissemination*, trans. Barbara Johnson (London: Athlone Press, 1981, pp. 61–171.
⁷¹ Roy Bhaskar, *Dialectic: the pulse of freedom* (London: Verso, 1993), p. 36.

Chapter 6

Points and Counterpoints: Between Hegel and Derrida

Arkady Plotnitsky

Différance, Points, Counterpoints

How is one to speak or to write, in a single essay, of the relationship between Derrida and Hegel, a relationship that absorbs several of Derrida's own books and many articles, and, in a certain sense, all of his work? The problem would be unsurmountable even if one could speak of this relationship as established or establishable, rather than as fluid and, at points, undecidable, which is in fact the case and which makes one think of this relationship as an instance of what Derrida calls *différance* – an equivocal (inter)play of proximities, differences, and interactions. This (undecidable) relationship pervades virtually the (untotalizable) totality of Derrida's work, along with and as part of the relationship between speech and writing, the exploration of which is Derrida's great project, in turn indissociable from Hegel – "the last philosopher of the book, the first thinker of writing", as Derrida calls him (*Of Grammatology*, 26). Indeed, in part for that very reason, Hegel's text itself would already pose monumental problems here. According to Derrida, writing in 1972, "elucidating the relationship with Hegel [is] a difficult labor, which for the most part remains before us, and which in a certain way is interminable, at least if one wishes to execute it rigorously and minutely" (*Positions*, 43). This is still the case, and one encounters many similar comments throughout Derrida's subsequent works. Derrida's own work is indissociable from and, in a certain sense, is an (interminable) entanglement with Hegel. I would argue that Hegel occupies a unique position for Derrida in this respect, at least in Derrida's earlier works, say, up to and including *Glas*, his most momentous treatment of Hegel. That is not to say that Derrida is simply Hegelian, any more than he is, say, simply Kantian or Heideggerian. First of all, at stake here is a *différance* between Derrida and Hegel (or Kant or Heidegger). Secondly, entanglements and/as *différance*-like relationships are abundant in Derrida and are germane to his work. One may think of Rousseau, Kant, Nietzsche, Husserl, Saussure, Heidegger, Freud, Bataille, Lacan, Blanchot, Levinas, and others, or many literary figures, such as Mallarmé, Joyce, and Genet, all of whom are linked to Hegel by Derrida. Genet is, of course, explicitly paired with Hegel, via many among the figures just mentioned, in *Glas*. Several other encounters-entanglements are crucial to the *différance* between Derrida and Hegel – one of Derrida–Bataille–Hegel in "From Restricted to General Economy: A Hegelianism without Reserve" (*Writing and Difference*), one of Derrida–Heidegger–Hegel in "Ousia and Gramma" (*Margins of Philosophy*), and one of Derrida–Heidegger–Freud in *The*

Post Card. Derrida's traversals of Saussure in "The Pit and the Pyramid" (*Margins*), Rousseau in *Of Grammatology* and related essays, and Mallarmé (via Plato) in "The Double Session" in *Dissemination* are also crucial here. One might think of some competition to Hegel in Derrida's work, such as Nietzsche, Freud, Bataille, Blanchot and, especially, Heidegger, whose meditation Derrida famously describes as "uncircumventable [incontournable]" (*Margins*, 22) and who might be seen as eventually supplanting Hegel in this respect in Derrida's later work; and Derrida, of course, often connects Heidegger and Hegel, as in "Ousia and Gramma" or (more implicitly) in *Of Spirit*, or elsewhere in his works. In any event, Derrida's text encompasses a second-order – *Glas*-like – entanglement of two already immense networks, Hegel's and his own. No lesser project than *Glas* may, then, be necessary in order to approach this immense entanglement between two immense texts, and ultimately no treatment – however long, however interminable – may be adequate in view of its *différance*-like nature.¹

"NOW, HOW AM I TO SPEAK OF the difference or *différance* between Derrida and Hegel? It is clear that it cannot be exposed. We can expose only what, at a certain moment, can become present, manifest; what can be shown, presented as a present, a being-present in its truth, the truth of a present or the presence of a present. However, if the *différance* between Hegel and Derrida [is] (I cross out "is") what makes the presentation of being-present of itself possible, it never presents itself as such. It is never given in the present or to anyone. Holding back and not exposing itself, it goes beyond the order of truth of this relationship on this specific point and in this determined way, yet is not itself concealed, as if it were something, a mysterious being, in the occult zone of a nonknowing. Any exposition would expose it to disappearing as a disappearance. It would risk appearing, thus disappearing."

One could hardly find a better description of the difficulty at issue, inevitably reaching a point at which it borders on and ultimately becomes a rigorous impossibility. The elaboration itself is, however, a virtually direct quotation of Derrida's elaboration on *différance* in "*Différance*," except that the word "*différance*" is replaced by "the *différance* between Derrida and Hegel" ("*Différance*," 134). *Différance* is a structure of very great formality and generality, perhaps the greatest possible generality, even though and because it makes all absolute formality or generality, or all absoluteness, themselves impossible. It follows that, while its inscription traverses, as it must, many proper names (from pre-Socratics to Heidegger and beyond), such a structure could not be unequivocally governed by any given proper name. Indeed, by definition, it could not be governed by or grounded in any single name or concept, be it Hegel, Heidegger, or Derrida, or even the name Being or the (un)name and (un)concept – neither a term nor a concept – of *différance* itself ("*Différance*," 158–59). And yet the same procedure of replacing or supplementing "*différance*" with "the *différance* between Derrida and Hegel" could be implemented throughout "*Différance*", and a similar point can be made about a number of Derrida's concepts and works, for example and especially, dissemination and most essays assembled in *Dissemination*.² *Glas* enacts a similar procedure explicitly in its pairing of Hegel with Genet and, implicitly, in its pairing of Derrida with both. The *différance* between Derrida and Hegel is, then, already inscribed in the signifying and conceptual texture of the essay – and hence in *différance* – at least in a certain reading.

Such an approach would not resolve most of the problems concerning writing (on) the *différance* between Derrida and Hegel since, as the passage just cited tells us, an inscription of *différance* itself poses at least as many problems as does the *différance* between Derrida and Hegel. This approach does, however, allow one to use another strategy – making points amidst the impossibility of making points, maintaining a fixed thesis, or, more generally, proceeding along the lines of "a [classical] philosophical discourse that operates on the basis of a principle, of postulates, axioms, and definitions and that moves according to the discursive lines of a linear order of reasons" ("*Différance*", 135).[3] "Everything [becomes] a matter of strategy and risk" (135). This need not mean that everything is left to chance, even though chance is irreducible. A much more complex (inter)play is at stake. As Derrida points out, announcing and joining two other major themes of his work, play and chance, "the concept of play [*jeu*] ... designates the unity of chance [*hasard*] and necessity in endless calculus" (135). Some of the risks involved are, then, calculated risks, although absolute security cannot be hoped for. An inevitable aspect of this strategy is, however, to snatch points from the jaws of the impossibility of making them, to snatch them from the chaos, or neither order nor chaos, of non-points.

The very metaphor of "point" – as punctuation, singularity, intersection (of lines), condensation, and so forth – suggests a quasi-geometrical image of the process at issue as giving a structure to an unstructured and only partially structured field. Deleuze and Guattari speak of "planes" (such as "planes of immanence"), meaning, in part via Bernhard Riemann's mathematical ideas, surfaces or manifolds upon which certain structures – topological, geometrical, algebraic, analytical, and so forth – can be introduced, including points themselves.[4] In their vision of philosophy as "the art of forming, inventing, and fabricating concepts, ... concepts that are always new" (*What is Philosophy?*, 2, 5), concepts could be (moving if necessary with "infinite" conceptual "speed") continuously and infinitely extended within themselves and in relation to the plane of immanence that defines a given philosophical field. Concepts slide from point to point, and define points – now, philosophical points – themselves. Continuity and/as infinity intensive (that is, within each interval) and extensive (that is, extending beyond any given limit) is crucial to Deleuze and Guattari's vision, in which the point, while a key concept, is seen as part of continuity and defined by Deleuze in *The Fold* via Leibniz and Paul Klee as a "nonconceptual concept of noncontradiction".[5] Following Nietzsche, Bataille, and Blanchot, in Derrida (and to a degree also in Hegel) one encounters a more discontinuous or rather more complementary – continuous and discontinuous – philosophical matrix, which is (conceptually) closer to quantum mechanics, especially in Niels Bohr's interpretation, rather than to continuous philosophical "geometry".[6] The concept of the point and its various "dimensions" (if one can apply this term to the dimensionless point) are, however, crucial to Derrida, in part for this very reason. His recent book of interviews is entitled *Points* and an earlier one is entitled *Positions*, and the metaphor or position is, of course, also a metaphor of the point. Both concepts, position and point, are crucial in inscribing the *différance* – the immense interplay of points and positions, concepts and planes or manifolds –

between Derrida and Hegel, who appears at many crucial points in both books and defines many crucial positions there.[7]

One might further extend the concept of "point" by way of the musical metaphor of counterpoint, even though in order to approach the *différance* between Derrida and Hegel (or *différance*, to begin with) one might want to invoke the most complex musical fabric or texture available. Such a concept can be correlated with the quasi-geometrical conceptualizations just considered, in part because the latter can in turn be related to (the "geometries" of) music, painting, or sculpture, or architecture – from (at least) the Baroque (Deleuze's great theme, via Leibniz) to modernism and postmodernism (and beyond), from El Greco and Bernini, great artists of the fold, to Klee, a key contemporary reference for Deleuze in his analysis of Leibniz in *The Fold*. In both cases – that of *différance* itself and that of the *différance* between Derrida and Hegel – at issue is a complex interplay of continuities and discontinuities, consonances and dissonances, harmonies, melodic and rhythmic structures, and so forth. Derrida sometimes appeals to "rhythm", including in the context of history and Hegel, and so does Deleuze throughout his work.[8] The richness of its structure enables Deleuze to develop the Baroque into a philosophical concept in his (and Guattari's) sense – a multilayered concept operating on a multilayered and multileveled manifold, or a family of manifolds. Indeed, along with *différance* and related conceptual clusters in Derrida, the Baroque may well be a unique concept of that type.[9] It combines the possibilities offered by Baroque mathematics and science (from Kepler to Leibniz) in its interactions with Baroque philosophy (from Leibniz to Hegel to Deleuze and Derrida), Baroque music (from Monteverdi and Bach to Schönberg and Boulez), Baroque architecture, sculpture and painting (from and before Michelangelo and Bernini to Klee and Mondrian), Baroque literature (from Dante and Shakespeare to Kafka and Joyce) and so forth.[10]

Deleuze sometimes uses both Leibniz and Spinoza against Hegel in this context. One may argue, however, that, thus understood, the Baroque as much, perhaps more, connects rather than dissociates them. By extension, as some of Deleuze's approaches to Kant would suggest, it also connects in a new way precritical (pre-Kantian) and critical (post-Kantian) philosophy. As a result, instead of being dissociated (as they often are), Deleuze and Derrida, too, may be connected, both, more predictably, via Nietzsche, Bataille, and Blanchot, and, more strangely, via Hegel. Through all these connections and by establishing them, the Baroque extends into an immense "chaosmos", to use Joyce's signifier, employed by both Deleuze and Derrida, and connecting (via many points, lines and surfaces) Hegel, Joyce, Deleuze, and Derrida.[11]

With these possibilities in mind, one may speak of a gigantic contrapuntal fabric of *différance* between Derrida and Hegel. I shall suggest here several specific aspects or points – or planes – of this contrapuntal *différance*. They include such topics as translation, proximity–distance economy, restricted and general economy, writing, and (en)closure. I shall address these topics alongside and as part of my argument concerning the special role of the *différance* between Derrida and Hegel in both "*Différance*" (the essay) and *différance* (the structure). Some of the elaborations to be discussed here are also indices of Derrida's major works on Hegel, most subsequent to "*Différance*," which – this is my point here –

is as much an inscription of *différance* as a kind of prolegomenon to Derrida's text on Hegel.

The Pit, The Pyramid, and the Tower

Hegel first overtly appears on the scene of *"Différance"* and/as "the scene of writing" by way of the quasi-Freudian or quasi-Lacanian analytics of a signifier, the key signifier (if it is even a signifier) of the essay – the famous inaudible "a" of Derridas *différance* – which makes the essay itself "the scene of writing".[12] This "a" can only be written, not heard (in French). As such it thematizes the complexities of writing and the equivocality, equi-vocality (in either sense) of its relation to speech and, at a certain point, the possibility of separating writing, gramma, from *phone*, from the spoken word. It is possible (perhaps) to speak of a letter, (perhaps) the first one – "I SHALL SPEAK, THEN, OF A LETTER, the first one" – Derrida says (*"Différance"*, 131). It is not possible, however, to speak of the "a" of *différance*, which impossibility allegorizes the impossibility of speaking and, at the limit, even of writing, inscribing *différance* "as such".[13] *Différance* entails a certain irreducible alterity. It is inaccessible to any representation, even the oblique' representation enacted by writing in Derrida's sense, which obliqueness is itself an effect of *différance* and surrounding structures, such as trace, dissemination, supplementarity, writing itself, and so forth (this list, by definition, cannot be closed). We cannot escape the effects of *différance*, even as *différance* "itself' escapes us. Derrida's "HOW SHALL I SPEAK OF the a of *différance*" (134), cited earlier, allegorizes this inescapable escapability. The "a" of *différance* thus also announces Derrida's essay "The Pit and the Pyramid: Introduction to a Hegelian Semiology". He writes:

> [The (inaudible) "a" of *différance*] is put forward by a silent mark, by a tacit monument, or, one might even say, by a pyramid – keeping in mind not only the capital form of the printed letter but also that passage from Hegel's *Encyclopedia* where he compares the body of the sign to an Egyptian pyramid. The a of *différance*, therefore, is not heard; it remains silent, secret, and discreet, like a tomb. It is a tomb that (provided one knows how to decipher its legend) is not far from signaling the death of the king. (*"Différance"*, 132)

While the passage is an index of an intersection-entanglement of a great many names, concepts, and texts, Hegel takes a singular place in it. The death of the king is, of course, the death of the philosopher-king of Plato's *Republic*. Perhaps even more so and more significantly, however, it is also the death of Hegel and of Hegelianism itself. But then it is also the death or, using the concept that Derrida is to develop later, the life-death (*la vie la mort*), of Hegel as Plato.[14] Dissemination will further extend the huge penumbra of the point made by this passage, a kind of pyramid standing upside down, a form of the Tower of Babel, symbolized or allegorized there by Mallarmé's "V" (239). "The Pit and the Pyramid" links or, again, exposes the irreducible entanglement of phenomenology and linguistics – of "Hegel" and "Saussure" – and irreducibly connects this entanglement to the question of writing.

The usage of the capital form of letter "A" is far more than an elegant graphic pun. First of all, it is the first letter of all Western alphabets, and, thus, a great "sign" of the very alphabetization of writing – of all alphabetism and alphabetocentrism, of alpha-centrism or (in its Hebrew form) aleph-centrism, or, which often amounts to the same, the alpha-omega centrism or/as apocalypticism.[15] These themes and their connections to such rubrics as phonocentrism, logocentrism, and so forth are crucial to "The Pit and the Pyramid" and to all of Derrida's work. As he says, "Doubtless this pyramidal silence of the graphic difference between the e and the a can function only within the system of phonetic [and hence, eventually, alphabetical] writing and within a language of grammar historically tied to phonetic writing and the whole culture that is unspeakable from it" (132). Hegel is a pyramidal or towering culmination of this culture, at least in the field of philosophy. All such towers, and all such pyramids, however, prove to be pyramids standing upside down, and are forms of the Tower of Babel. Derrida's point on upside-down writing in *The Post Card* (194) is deeply related to this imagery and the configuration behind it, expanded, ever more radically, throughout Derrida's work, as in the famous Plato–Socrates reversal on *The Post Card* or Hegel's preface-postface economy in "Hors Livre" in *Dissemination*. Derrida's analysis exposes writing (in Derrida's sense) and/as the work of divergent translation(s) within the supposed classical pyramidal order of speech (or thought) and its classical relations to writing, as a representation of speech (in turn representing thought). At stake here is also a problematization and a deconstruction of the concept of (purely) phonetic writing, which does not exist in its pure form but of which alphabetic writing is claimed to be the capitalization or, again, culmination – from ALPHA to OMEGA. Instead it, too, is another Tower of Babel, a conglomerate of irreducibly diverging significations-translations, as "The Pit and the Pyramid" and related works show so powerfully. To begin with, "a" is the first letter only "if we are to believe the alphabet and most of the speculations that have concerned itself with it" ("*Différance*", 131). This deconstruction problematizes the distinction between hieroglyphic – pyramidal, silent – writing and the phonetic writing – writing that speaks, writing with a voice.

Hegel's name is sometimes pronounced in French as aigle – eagle – which word, too, begins with an "a", while making the difference (*différance*?) between Hegel and Aigle just as inaudible as that between difference and *différance*. Hegel is the Aigle, with a capital "A", to whom he is often compared – the symbol of many an empire, above all the empire of philosophy itself. Derrida's elaboration may be seen as announcing the famous opening of *Glas*, which echoes it on many points and along many lines:

> Who, he? His name so strange. From the eagle [*aigle*] it draws imperial or historic power. Those who still pronounce his name like the French (there are some) are ludicrous only up to a certain point: the restitution (semantically infallible for those who have read him a little – but only a little) of magisterial coldness and imperturbable seriousness, the eagle caught in ice and frost, *glas* and *gel* [gel].

Let the emblanched [*emblémi*] philosopher be so congealed [*figé*]. (*Glas*, 1a). It is impossible ever to make Hegel congeal completely, to make him a pyramidal A-shaped monument, to silence him in a tomb or make him a tomb, a/the tomb of a/the philosopher-king. Hegel is slowly uncongealed in "*Différance*", *Glas*, and throughout Derrida's text by and into a *différance*-like movement. "What differs? Who differs? What is *différance*?" – Derrida asks in "*Différance*" (145). Who differs? Who is he (Hegel)? Who are we? These are perhaps the same questions, certainly part of the same *différance* and of the "same" as *différance* with an a. "Who, he? His name so strange", just like the (un)name of *différance* or *glas*. "Some concepts must be indicated by an extraordinary and sometimes even barbarous or shaking words, whereas others make do with an ordinary word that is filled with harmonics so distant that it risks being imperceptible to a nonphilosophical ear. Some concepts call for archaisms, and others for neologisms", Deleuze and Guattari write (*What is Philosophy*, 8). All these features come together in Derrida's names – Hegel/Aigle, *glas*, *différance*, ... – and their *différance* from, their counterpoints with, their life-death in, each other.

Translations

Hegel's name re-enters the scene of "*Différance*" at the point of a potential question, the question concerning names: "Given this (active) movement of the (production) of *différance* without origin, could we not, quite simply and without any neographism, call it differentiation?" Derrida points out first that "among other confusions, such a word would suggest some organic unity, some primordial and homogenous unity, that would eventually come to be divided up and take on difference as an event" ("*Différance*", 143). The latter economy is sometimes associated with Hegel and is part of – or is productive of – certain forms of Hegelianism, which one should distinguish from Hegel. An economy of that type is, however, not something that Derrida attributes to Hegel. Instead, Derrida proceeds via Alexandre Koyré's translation/reading of Hegel, while anticipating his own discussion of the workings of *différance* (as "the unconscious") in Nietzsche and Freud in a counterpoint with Hegel's (or, again, a certain Hegelian) economy of consciousness later in the essay (148–52). He writes:

> Koyré cited long passages from the Jena Logic in German and gives his own translation. On two occasions in Hegel's text he encounters the expression "differente Beziehung." This word (different), whose root is Latin [hence closer to French and the double of different/deferred of *différance*], is extremely rare in German and also, I believe, in Hegel, who instead uses *verschieden* or *ungleich*, calling difference *Untershied* and qualitative variety *Verschiedenheit*. In the Jena Logic, he uses the word different precisely at the point where he deals with time and the present [in speaking of "an absolutely different relation of the simple"] ... Koyré specifies in a striking note: "Different relation: Differente Beziehung. We could say: differentiating relation." And on the following page, from another text of Hegel, we can read: "Diese Beziehung ist Gegenwart, als eine differente Beziehung (This relation is [the] present, as a different relation). There is another note by Koyré: "The term 'different' is taken here in an active sense." ("*Différance*", 144)

Koyré's "translation" allows Derrida to make several key points concerning the effects and usages of *différance*. His first point concerns new possibilities of translation and reading of Hegel, at least in French, but also, by a reverse traffic, in German. He writes: "Writing 'differing' or '*différance*' (with an a) would have had the utility of making it possible to translate Hegel on precisely this point with no further qualifications – and it is a quite decisive point in his text. The translation would be, as it always should be, the transformation of one language by another" (144). Of course, a translation not only "should be" but always is "a transformation of one language by another". Derrida, however, imparts to this proposition a more active connotation of translation under the conditions of *différance*, of the irreducibility of the effects of *différance* (as the efficacy of proximities, differences, interactions) in translation. These effects allow one to (re)translate and to (re)read Hegel at this or that historical point (here, not insignificantly, in 1968). As any translation, this one is already irreducibly entangled (in a double bind) with a reading of Hegel. This entanglement is subject to what Derrida calls supplementarity, which may be seen as a translation of Freud's *Nachträglichkeit*. Supplementarity is defined in *Speech and Phenomena* as follows, "By delayed reaction, a possibility produces that to which it is said to be added on" (98).[16] The irreducibility of supplementarity (in its various forms) in translation amplifies the view of translation as correlatively interactive with writing in Derrida's sense, an idea developed throughout Derrida's subsequent work. From this perspective, writing itself could be seen as translation without (absolute) original, while philosophy becomes suspended between translation and creation of concepts, such as those of Hegel and Derrida's neither terms nor concepts.[17] Derrida's translation would (re)produce Hegelian difference not as the organic unity that he associates with "differentiation," but instead as something that is much closer to *différance*, on nearly every point of its inscription. How close is, of course, a crucial question. It may be asked, or answered, in both directions (moving from Hegel to Derrida or from Derrida to Hegel) depending on one's reading of both. Derrida's answer is a certain proximity–distance economy.

Proximities–Distances

Derrida introduces his proximity–distance economy – a displacement of Hegel that is both infinitesimal and radical – immediately after the elaboration on translation just considered:

> Naturally, I maintain that the word "*différance*" can be used in other ways, too; first of all, because it denotes not only the activity of primordial difference but also the temporalizing detour of deferring. It has, however, an even more important usage. Despite the very profound affinities that *différance* thus written has with Hegelian speech (as it should be read), it can, at a certain point, not exactly break with it, but rather work a sort of displacement with regard to it. A definite rupture with Hegelian language would make no sense, nor would it be at all likely; but this displacement is both infinitesimal and radical. ("*Différance*", 135)

This is a crucial point (in either sense), for while it or a similar point may in principle be argued for the role of other figures in Derrida, Derrida himself never makes it except in relation to Hegel. I would suggest that, while often in turn *différance*-like, Derrida's relationships with other figures that can be invoked here, including Heidegger, are structured differently. Derrida reiterates the point in these very words in *Positions* (43–44) and elsewhere in his works. If, then, one proceeds by reading and following Hegel's text very closely, one can, at a certain point, displace his conceptual chains or networks – ever so slightly, infinitesimally. The results, however, are radical, indeed so radical that if *différance* could be defined (in truth it cannot) it would be defined as at the limit (and as the limit) of this process:

> If there were a single definition of *différance* it would be the interruption, the destruction of the Hegelian *relève* (that is, *Aufhebung*) wherever it operates. What is at stake here is enormous [*L'enjeu est ici énorme*]. I emphasize the Hegelian *Aufhebung*, such as it is interpreted by a certain Hegelian discourse, for it goes without saying that the double meaning of *Aufhebung* [i.e. that of negating and conserving or/as superseding] could be written otherwise. Whence its proximity to all operations conducted against Hegel's dialectical speculation. (*Positions*, 40–41)

Yet, the displacement is also so infinitesimal that one needs to traverse much, perhaps all, of Derrida's text in order to understand, if not to discern, it. One of Derrida's approaches to this double-structure is via the question of restricted and general economy, as defined by Bataille.

"From Restricted to General Economy"

Introduced by analogy with (the science of) political economy, "general economy" is understood by Bataille as theory or "science," (as opposed to the "economic" system or configuration that such a theory would account for). It is opposed by Bataille to classical or "restricted" economies, such as that of Hegel's philosophy (in this reading) or Marx's political economy. Such theories would aim or claim to contain or control, at least in principle, (all) indeterminacy, alterity, loss, and non-selective (excessive) accumulation of or within the systems they describe. By contrast, while remaining rigorously scientific, general economies would expose that such, from the classical perspective "negative", structures are irreducible. Hegel's economy of the negative is a classical or more classical response to this non-classical situation.[18] The "science" of general economy may be seen as pursuing analyses of non-classical (general-economic) efficacity of the processes that classical theories (restricted economies) understand in such terms or term-clusters as meaning, presence, and truth; full consciousness and self-consciousness; the possibility of unconditionally grounding or centering interpretation or theory; the possibility of interpretive and theoretical gains without accompanying losses; the possibility of a fully coherent unity of knowledge; the possibility of projects based on these assumptions, and so forth. These configurations are all complicit within what Derrida terms the metaphysics of presence, logocentrism, or, following Heidegger, ontotheology – a powerful and systematic unity that defines the history of Western philosophy, but is operative well beyond its limits. According to Bataille:

> The science of relating the object of thought to sovereign moments in fact is only a general economy which envisages the meaning of these objects in relation to each other and finally in relation to the loss of meaning. ... The general economy, in the first place, makes apparent that excesses of energy are produced, which by definition cannot be utilized. The excessive energy can only be lost without the slightest aim, consequently without any meaning. This useless, senseless loss is sovereignty. (*Oeuvres Complètes* 5:215–16, emphasis added)

What Bataille calls "sovereignty" here is expressly juxtaposed by him to, or is a "translation" or/as ambivalent displacement of, the Hegelian mastery (*Herrschaft*) or a correlative economy in Marx. Both Derrida's *différance* and Bataille's sovereignty translate Hegel's *Herrschaft* and each other. The connections of Bataille's concept of general economy and of his philosophical and textual practice to Hegel are multi-leveled and complex. Some among them – such as those to Hegel's dialectic of master and slave – are immediately apparent here. Others – such as those related to other dimensions of sovereignty and sacrifice – would require a more complex tracing. Derrida's relationships with Bataille is a huge topic in its own right. Given my limits here, I shall take a short-cut, via Derrida's extraordinary elaboration in "*Différance*", where he writes:

> Here we touch on the point of greatest obscurity, on the very enigma of *différance*, on that which divides its very concept by a strange cleavage. We must not hasten to decide. How are we to think simultaneously, on the one hand, *différance* as the economic detour which, in the element of the same, always aims at coming back to the pleasure or the presence that have been deferred by (conscious or unconscious) calculation, and, on the other hand, *différance* as the relation to an impossible presence, as expenditure without reserve, as the irreparable loss of presence, the irreversible usage of energy, that is, as the death drive, and as the entirely other [*tout-autre*] relationship that apparently interrupts every economy? It is evident – and this is evidence itself – that the economical and the noneconomical, the same and the entirely other, etc., cannot be thought together. If *différance* is unthinkable in this way, perhaps we should not hasten to make it evident, in the philosophical element of evidentiality which would make short work of dissipating the mirage and illogicalness of *différance* and would do so with the infallibility of calculus that we are well acquainted with, having precisely recognized their place, necessity, and function in the structure of *différance*. What would be accounted for philosophically here has already been taken into account in the system of *différance* as it is here being calculated. Elsewhere, in a reading of Bataille, I have attempted to indicate what might come of a rigorous and, in a new sense, "scientific" relating of the "restricted economy" that takes no part in expenditure without reserve, death, opening itself to nonmeaning, etc., to a general economy that takes into account the nonreserve, that keeps in reserve the nonreserve, if it can be put thus. I am speaking of a relationship between a *différance* that can make a profit on its investment and a *différance* that misses its profit, the investiture of presence that is pure and without loss here being confused with absolute loss, with death. Through such a relating of a restricted and a general economy the very project of philosophy, under the privileged heading of Hegelianism, is displaced and reinscribed. The *Aufhebung* – *la relève* – is constrained into writing itself otherwise. Or perhaps simply into

writing itself. Or, better, into taking account of its consumption of writing. (*Margins*, 19; "*Différance*", 150–51; translation modified)[19]

This passage, too, could be read as a translation-transformation of Hegel. Following Bataille, Blanchot, Heidegger, and several others, it offers a general-economic (re)reading of Hegel's famous passage on "tarrying with the negative," or of the conclusion of the *Phenomenology*, where Hegel arguably comes the closest to general economy (18–19, 491–93). While remaining in an infinitesimal proximity to it, the (general) economy at stake here radically refigures Hegel's Spirit, Geist, or the Ghost (Specter) of Geist. This refiguring is extended by Derrida in *Glas*, *Of Spirit*, and, via Marx, in *Specters of Marx*, and again, in a certain sense, throughout his work. At stake here is also a "science" that represents the relationship between that which is representable in the classical sense and that which is unrepresentable by any means, classical or not, or through any concept (for example, that of the absolutely unrepresentable), but to which one can relate – obliquely, but rigorously – by means of a general economy.

It also follows, however, that, instead of abandoning the classical (classical theory, representation, and so forth), this approach makes the classical and the non-classical irreducibly interactive within a non-classical framework, such as Derrida's, or Bataille's and Nietzsche's, just as restricted and general economies themselves are always interactive. Otherwise (the radical inaccessibility of) the non-classical would be inaccessible, or accessible only as absolutely inaccessible, which is still too accessible, and, hence, is not radical enough. Derrida's next elaboration in "*Différance*" inscribes *différance* as a radical alterity "as concerns every possible mode of presence" (*Margins*, 20–21). This alterity cannot be conceived as an absolute alterity, such as that, say, of Kantian things-in-themselves – anymore than being available to conceptual mastery, such as that, say, of Hegelian dialectics and the *Aufhebung* (in a certain reading of Kant and Hegel, since Kant's and Hegel's concepts have greater complexity). Derrida also invokes "radical alterity" in the context of the question of materiality, Marxism, and Hegel, and referring again to "From Restricted to General Economy" (*Positions*, 64).[20] Even if imperceptible to Hegel himself, this radical alterity and other general-economic dislocations inhabit – and inhibit – Hegel's economy. "Hegel" – Derrida says – "saw this without seeing, revealed it by concealing it" (*Writing and Difference*, 260). By doing so, however, he also opened the way to a different form of Hegelianism, "a Hegelianism without reserve."

Writing and (En)closures

"'Hegelianism'," according to Derrida, is "the finest scar" of a "battle" against writing (*Of Grammatology*, 99). Emerging through a deconstruction of the classical concept of writing as a representation of speech, a (general-economic) "science" of writing was originally proposed by Derrida under the name "grammatology" in *Of Grammatology* and other earlier texts. Along with other "positive" sciences this "science" is juxtaposed to classical, particularly Saussurean, linguistics as the science of speech conceived of in a metaphysical opposition to writing.[21] In privileging speech over writing, this opposition characterizes virtually all classical philosophy as ontotheology and the metaphysics of presence, with which linguistics thus becomes complicit. If, however, this concept of writing is shown to be uncritical, the same is also true of the classical concept of speech. Derrida's economy of writing deconstructs and refigures both within (and by establishing) a certain shifting *différance* rather than creating a rigid hierarchy between them. Derrida demonstrates how what he calls writing emerges in the place to which classical theories – whether in philosophy, linguistics, anthropology, or elsewhere – assign the denomination of language as speech. The resulting new concept, or "neither a word nor a concept", of writing can no longer be understood as a representation of speech, as the latter concept and all other classical concepts involved are in turn transformed: "It is not a question of resorting to the same concept of writing and of simply inverting the dissymmetry that now has become problematical. It is a question, rather, of producing a new concept of writing" (*Positions*, 26). Elsewhere, Derrida describes the "nuclear traits of all writing" (in this new sense) as follows:

> (1) the break with the horizon of communication as the communication of consciousness and presences, and as the linguistic and semantic transport of meaning; (2) the subtraction of all writing from the semantic horizon or the hermeneutic horizon, at least as a horizon of meaning, let itself be punctured by writing; (3) the necessity of, in a way, separating the concept of *polisemia* [a controlled plurality of meaning] from the concept I have elsewhere named dissemination, which is also the concept of writing; (4) the disqualification or the limit of the concept of the "real" or "linguistic" context, whose theoretical determination or empirical saturation [is], strictly speaking, rendered impossible or insufficient by writing. (*Margins*, 316)

No less, perhaps more, than *différance*, dissemination, which Derrida also calls "seminal *différance*" (*Positions*, 45), is connected to Hegel throughout, and often (perhaps always) analogously to, and interactively with, the way that *différance* is here connected to Hegel, "the first thinker of writing".[22] Hegel is not the only name of the problem of writing, but one of the greatest, perhaps along with Plato and Rousseau. In *The Truth of Painting* Derrida "name[s] the necessity of deconstruction" with "[the] proper name Hegel", and speaks of Hegel's "determinant role in the construction of the French University and its philosophical institution" (19; emphasis added). Hegel is the name and the problem looming over our theoretical, historical and political discourse. The question is whether one can ever leave Hegel behind and exceed the Hegelian (en)closure or, more generally (but interactively), what Derrida sees as the (en)closure (*clôture*) of metaphysics.

The question of closure is only marginally mentioned in "*Différance*" (131), but it is crucial to the (joined) thematics of *différance* and of the *différance* between Derrida and Hegel. The closure of metaphysics or philosophy in Derrida designates our dependence on language, concepts, and strategies developed throughout the history of philosophy – as the metaphysics of presence – but operative elsewhere as well, which extension compels one to speak of the closure of philosophy.[23] According to Derrida, this dependence is fundamental and irreducible. In many ways, Derrida's deconstruction might be seen as an investigation of this closure, which may indeed be an interminable project, for "that which is held within the delimited closure may continue indefinitely" (*Positions*,

13; translation modified).[24] Although the term "closure" would naturally suggest conclusion, end, or termination, the closure of metaphysics as understood by Derrida, also implies an "enclosure" and interminability within it, suggested by the double meaning of the French "*clôture*" (and in truth of the English "closure" as well). Derrida distinguishes the end and the closure from the outset of his project, as in *Of Grammatology* (4) or *Positions* (13–14).

While the question of the closure of metaphysics or philosophy may not be strictly Hegel's question, it is close enough to Hegel to be a Hegelian question, in particular in the context of the question of history and of the end of history[25] In *Of Grammatology*, Derrida sums up the Hegelian economy as follows: "Hegel was already caught up in this game... He undoubtedly summed up the entire philosophy of the logos. He determined ontology as absolute logic; he assembled all the delimitations of being as presence" (*Of Grammatology*, 24; translation modified).[26] Hegel summed up philosophy in its determination as ontotheology and/as the metaphysics of presence, and, as "the first thinker of writing," brought it to the threshold of general economy and, at certain points, made it cross this threshold. As a result, it becomes possible to speak of a post-Hegelian closure – the closure of philosophy, as well as, perhaps the more "primordial," closure of presence itself. *Différance* is seen by Derrida "as the strategic note or connection – relatively and provisionally privileged – which indicated the closure of presence, together with the closure of the conceptual order and denomination, a closure that is effected in the functioning of traces" ("*Différance*", 131).[27] This statement is made overtly in conjunction with "the ontic-ontological difference in Heidegger" (130), and the question of closure is irreducibly Heideggerian.[28] However, as must be clear from the passage from *Of Grammatology*, cited above, and as "Ousia and Gramma" and other works would further demonstrate, Hegel's work is crucial to this joint thematics of the closure of presence and the closure of philosophy as the metaphysics of presence – to the point of allowing one to see this closure as Hegelian or post-Hegelian. It could be seen as such not because it did not exist before Hegel (it has no more an absolute beginning than absolute end) but because, if without quite realizing it, in his attempt to define the conceptual and historical functioning of philosophy itself, Hegel instead inscribed the functioning of the closure of philosophy alongside the similarly unperceived (or insufficiently perceived) functioning of writing. He is the first thinker of this closure in the same sense that he is the first thinker of writing; and it could be shown that the question of writing and the question of closure are indissociable. What is claimed by Hegel for philosophy can only be claimed for a certain closure of philosophy as the metaphysics of presence. In an infinitesimal proximity to and a radical difference from Hegel, the concept of the closure of philosophy replaces Hegel's concept of philosophy as having (or, at a certain point, acquiring) the central role in the history of knowledge.

Derrida's analysis of closure does, however, pose the question of the difference or *différance* between Heidegger's "end" and the "de(con)struction [Destruktion]" of metaphysics, and Derrida's "closure" and "deconstruction" of metaphysics. Partly for this reason, the questions of the closure of presence and of the closure of metaphysics are often considered by Derrida in conjunction with Heidegger. These questions, however, must be asked and, in all rigor, perhaps could only be asked via Hegel. While these "triangular" questions cannot be addressed here, in more general terms what would be the relation of a deconstructive text, such as Derrida's, to the text of philosophy and its margins? A necessary relation? A unique relation? How would this relation define a relation, as that of a certain "agon" or that of "friendship", between Derrida and Hegel?[29]

Philosophy is an extraordinarily capacious and massive force or rather field of forces, both heterogenous and unified. This force has enabled the power and extension of its closure, arguably a historically unique closure of that type. Within the closure of philosophy and Hegelianism, Derrida conceives of this very continuity as the closure of philosophy – of its concepts, strategies, and many other things that philosophy offers to us and imposes upon us. All these terms – history, continuity, transformation, break, or closure itself – do belong to this closure. But, as Derrida often points out, philosophy cannot quite own them, either, and they have been transformed a great deal inside and, or, as ... (other conjunctions are possible) outside philosophy along with the boundaries between – and within – the fields where these concepts function. But then, how far does the closure of philosophy (as the metaphysics of presence) extend? Derrida's work poses a fundamental question in this respect – one of the most radical questions opened by his work – on the way to a new Tower or rather Towers of Babel. Building this City of Babel would require all the technology we possess, classical and non-classical, conceptual or strictly technological (be it word-processors or whatever). Perhaps, and, in a certain sense, definitionally, no technology or/as nontechnology – nothing, including nothingness itself – will ever enable us to quite succeed.[30] These new technologies may, however, allow us to explore and create, with, among others, Hegel and Derrida, the field of philosophy not as ontotheology or the metaphysics of presence but as an irreducibly heterogenous and undecidable field of the relationships between translation and creation, the conceptual and the unconceptual, the accessible and the inaccessible, the possible and the impossible, which incessantly, interminably pass into – translate and create – each other, as do Hegel and Derrida.

Purdue University, West Lafayette, IN

Notes

[1] The list of Derrida's relevant works and elaborations would be long and, at the limit, would, again, encompass all of his work. It is virtually impossible to list the innumerable secondary commentaries. I have considered the subject in several previously published studies, to which I permit myself to refer here, and which are listed in the bibliography to this essay, along with several commentaries on Hegel's and Derrida's own works that I have used in this essay.

[2] There are, of course, as there must be given the *différance*-like economy at issue, concepts that irreducibly differentiate Hegel and Derrida – especially, "undecidability," introduced by Derrida, by analogy with Kurt Gödel's undecidability in mathematical logic, in *Dissemination* (219), and, one could argue, not found in Hegel. The limits of this essay prevent me from considering undecidability in detail.

[3] On "athesis" see especially *The Post Card*, 260–73.

[4] See their *What is Philosophy?* Their vision is not without its Hegelian genealogy, and one might even see it as a translation-transformation of Hegel's economy of the

Concept [*Begriff*] in the *Phenomenology* or later that of the Idea. (Cf. *What is Philosophy?*, 11–12). These mathematical ideas are used here only metaphorically or as philosophical concepts. No claim is made as to a mathematical or scientific functioning of the structures involved.

[5] See Deleuze, *The Fold*, 14.

[6] I have discussed Bohr's ideas in these contexts in *Complementarity* and *In the Shadow of Hegel*. On philosophical "geometry" in Derrida, see his remarks in *Points* (223). The question of geometry in Husserl plays an important role in Derrida's work on Husserl, which can be considered in this context as well. See, again, *Points* (223).

[7] Derrida's concept of "space" as *khora* developed in *Khora* is also of considerable interest here, as are many earlier elaborations on (and problematizing of) spatiality and temporality in *"Différance"*, *Positions*, and *Of Grammatology*, or, again, in *Points*.

[8] Cf. his elaborations in *Positions* (58) and "Choreographies", which can, again, be linked to *Khora* in this context.

[9] Cf. *The Fold*, 32–34.

[10] Many of these connections are suggested by Deleuze in *The Fold*.

[11] It would not be possible here to trace the relevant Joycean trajectories in Derrida's texts. Key works here include, "Violence and Metaphysics" (*Writing and Difference*, 153, 32122n.92) and *Ulysse gramophone*.

[12] So is, of course, Derrida's essay on Freud, "Freud and the Scene of Writing" (*Writing and Difference*). It, too, has important Hegelian points or planes, linked to the economy of *différance*, as do all Derrida's works on Freud, most recently *Mal d'archive*. Cf. also Bernard Stiegler's discussion of Freud's concept of history, via Derrida, in "Persephone, Oedipus, Epimetheus" (97–112), which, however, bypasses Hegel.

[13] I also refer here to Paul de Man's concept of allegory and its connection to both Hegel and Derrida, and the *différance* between Hegel and Derrida, and Derrida's discussion of de Man's analysis of Hegel in *Memoires for Paul de Man*.

[14] This concept is developed by Derrida in "Living On: Border Lines" and his other works on Blanchot (in *Parages*).

[15] The theme of apocalypse is explored, including in the Hegelian context, in several of Derrida's works, such as, to name only some of them, *The Post Card*, *Parages*, *Of Spirit*, *Glas*, and "Of the Apocalyptic Tone Newly Adopted in Philosophy".

[16] On supplement, see also his discussion of Rousseau in *Of Grammatology* and "Freud and the Scene of Writing."

[17] For Derrida's approaches to translation, see "Living On: Border Lines" and "Des Tours de Babel" (*Psyché*).

[18] "From Restricted to General Economy" clearly suggests this point throughout.

[19] I use here mostly Alan Bass's version in *Margins*.

[20] Cf. also his comments on Levinas in *"Différance"* (*Margins*, 21) and throughout "Violence and Metaphysics," and many other elaborations in *Of Grammatology*, *Writing and Difference*, *Positions*, and many other works. See also "The Almost Nothing of the Unpresentable" (in *Points*).

[21] See the chapter "*Of Grammatology* as a Positive Science" (*Of Grammatology*, 74–93).

[22] It is possible to undertake an analysis of dissemination and the key works involved, such as *Dissemination*, parallel to the analysis of *différance* pursued by this essay.

[23] This qualification "as the metaphysics of presence" is crucial. As Derrida often points out and as his work examplified, it is not possible to ever unequivocally – un-undecidably – establish what constitutes philosophy as against non-philosophy, what is inside and what is outside philosophy, draw all its boundaries (within and without), and so forth.

[24] Derrida's elaborations on closure are numerous and complex – irreducibly nonsimple – and require a careful analysis, which cannot be undertaken here. The question is rarely addressed in commentaries on Derrida, numerous as they are. It is considered, relatively briefly, by Rodolphe Gasché in *The Tain of the Mirror: Derrida and the Philosophy of Reflection* (which also offers a discussion of Derrida and Hegel) and, extensively, in the context of Levinas and the question of ethics by Simon Critchley in *The Ethics of Deconstruction: Derrida and Levinas*. I have considered this question of closure in detail in *Reconfigurations* (194–212), *In the Shadow of Hegel* (115–25), and *Complementarity* (225–69), and "Closing the Eye".

[25] Contrary to some earlier, and some continuing and persistent misunderstanding along different (and sometimes opposing) lines – from attributing to him a classical, even idealist, view of history as "the history of meaning" to attributing to him a "rejection of history" (*Positions*, 50) – the question of history has preoccupied Derrida from his earliest work on Husserl to his most recent works, in particular, in the context of the end of history, in *Specters of Marx*. Derrida elaborates on these issues at some length in both *Positions* and *Points*.

[26] See also *Speech and Phenomena* (101–02) and "Ousia and Gramma".

[27] Along with the original opening of the essay, this elaboration is omitted in the version published in *Margins*.

[28] Cf. Philippe Lacoue-Labarth's discussion in *Heidegger, Art and Politics*.

[29] Beyond Derrida's *Politiques de l'amitié*, I refer here to both Blanchot's (*The Infinite Conversation*) and Deleuze and Guattari's (*What is Philosophy?*) discussion of the concept of "friendship" and its role in philosophy. I have considered this question in "Closing the Eye: Hegel, Derrida, and the Closure of Philosophy."

[30] "The question concerning technology", to use Heidegger's famous title and phrase here, has been a major subject of Derrida's work, from the earliest to the most recent, including in his analysis of Hegel, as, for example, in his discussion of the question of machine in Hegel in "The Pit and the Pyramid". I have considered these issues in *Reconfigurations* (297–324).

Bibliography

Bataille, Georges. *Oeuvres complètes*. Paris: Gallimard, 1970–88.
Blanchot, Maurice. *L'Entretien infini*. Paris: Gallimard, 1969. Translated by Susan Hanson as *The Infinite Conversation*. Minneapolis, Minn: University of Minnesota Press, 1993.
Bennington, Geoffrey and Jacques Derrida. *Jacques Derrida*. Paris: Editions du Seuil, 1991. Translated by Geoffrey Bennington as *Jacques Derrida*. Chicago: University of Chicago Press, 1993
Critchley, Simon. *The Ethics of Deconstruction: Derrida and Levinas*. Oxford: Blackwell, 1992.
Deleuze, Gilles. *Le Pli: Leibniz et le baroque*. Paris: Les Editions de Minuit, 1988. Translated by Tom Conley as *The Fold: Leibniz and the Baroque*. Minneapolis, Minn.: University of Minnesota Press, 1993.
Deleuze, Gilles, and Felix Guattari. *Ou'est-ce que la philosophie?* Paris: Editions de Minuit, 1972. Translated by Hugh Tomplinson and Graham Burchell as *What is Philosophy?* New York: Columbia University Press, 1994.
De Man, Paul. *Blindness and Insight*. Minneapolis: University of Minnesota Press, 1983.
–. "Hegel and the Sublime". In *Displacements*, ed. Mark Krupnick. Bloomington: Indiana University Press, 1987.

—. "Sign and Symbol in Hegel's Aesthetics". *Critical Inquiry* (Summer 1982): 761–75.
Derrida, Jacques. "L'Age de Hegel". *GREPH. Qui a peur de la philosophie*. Paris: Flammarion, 1977, 73–107.
—. "Of the Apocalyptic Tone Newly Adopted in Philosophy". In *Derrida and Negative Theology*, ed. Harold Coward and Tobey Foshay. Albany, NY: SUNY Press, 1992.
—. *La Carte postale: De Socrate à Freud et au-delà*. Paris: Flammarion, 1980. Translated by Alan Bass as *The Post Card: From Socrates to Freud and Beyond*. Chicago: University of Chicago Press, 1987.
—. "Choreographies". *Diacritics* 12 (1982): 66–76.
—. *De la grammatologie*. Paris: Editions de Minuit, 1967. Translated by Gayatri C. Spivak as *Of Grammatology*. Baltimore: Johns Hopkins University Press, 1976.
—. *De l'esprit: Heidegger et la question*. Paris: Editions Galilee, 1987. Translated by Geoffrey Bennington and Rachel Bowlby as *Of Spirit: Heidegger and the Question*. Chicago: University of Chicago Press, 1989.
—. "La '*différance*'". *Bulletin de la Société Française de la Philosophie* 62, no. 3 (July–September 1968): 73–101. Translated by David B. Allison as "*Différance*." In *Speech and Phenomena And Other Essays on Husserl's Theory of Science*. Translated by David B. Allison. Evanston, Ill.: Northwestern University Press, 1973.
—. *La Dissémination*. Paris: Éditions du Seuil, 1972. Translated by Barbara Johnson as *Dissemination*. Chicago: University of Chicago Press, 1981.
—. *L'Écriture et la différence*. Paris: Editions du Seuil, 1967. Translated by Alan Bass as *Writing and Difference*. Chicago: University of Chicago Press, 1978.
—. Trans. and intro. *Edmund Husserl, L'Origine de la géométrie*. Paris: Presses Universitaires de France, 1962. Translated by John P. Leavy, Jr., as *Edmund Husserl's Origin of Geometry: An Introduction*. Stony Brook, NY: Nicolas Hays, 1978.
—. *Glas*. Paris: Galilée, 1974. Translated by John P. Leavey, Jr., and Richard Rand as *Glas*. Lincoln: University of Nebraska Press, 1986.
—. "Living On: Border Lines". Translated by James Hulbert. In Harold Bloom et al., *Deconstruction and Criticism*. New York: Seabury Press, 1979.
—. *Khora*. Paris: Galilée, 1993.
—. *Mal d'archive*. Paris: Galilée, 1995.
—. *Marges de la philosophie*. Paris: Editions de Minuit, 1972. Translated by Alan Bass as *Margins of Philosophy*. Chicago: University of Chicago Press, 1982.
—. *Memoires for Paul de Man*. Trans. Cecile Lindsay, Jonathan Culler, and Eduardo Cadava. New York: Columbia University Press, 1986.
—. *Parages*. Paris: Galilée, 1986.
—. *Points de suspension. Entretiens*. Paris: Galilée, 1992. Translated by Peggy Kamuf and others as *Points*. Stanford, Ca.: Stanford University Press, 1995.
—. *Politiques de l'amitié*. Paris: Galilée, 1995.
—. *Positions*. Paris: Éditions de Minuit, 1972. Translated by Alan Bass as *Positions*. Chicago: University of Chicago Press, 1981.
—. *Psyché: Inventions de l'autre*. Paris: Galilée, 1987.
—. *Spectres de Marx*. Paris: Galilée, 1993. Translated by Peggy Kamuf as *Specters of Marx*. New York: Routledge, 1994.
—. *Ulysse gramophone: Deux mots pour Joyce*. Paris: Galilée, 1987.
—. *La Vérité en peinture*. Paris: Flammarion, 1978. Translated by Geoffrey Bennington and Ian Mcleod as *The Truth in Painting*. Chicago: University of Chicago Press, 1987.

–. *La Voix et le phénomène*. Paris: Presses Universitaires de France, 1967. Translated by David B. Allison as *Speech and Phenomena*. In *Speech and Phenomena And Other Essays on Husserl's Theory of Science*. Translated by David B. Allison. Evanston, Ill.: Northwestern University Press, 1973.

Gasché, Rodolphe. The *Tain of The Mirror: Derrida and the Philosophy of Reflection*. Cambridge, Mass.: Harvard University Press, 1986.

Hegel, Georg Wilhelm Friedrich. Gesammelte Werke. Hamburg: Felix Meiner, 1968.

–. *Hegel's Science of Logic*. Translated by A.V. Miller. Atlantic Highlands, NJ: Humanities Press International, 1990.

–. *Werke in 20 Bänden*. Edited by Eva Moldenhauer and Karl Markus Michel. Frankfurt am Main: Suhrkamp, 1970–1971.

–. *Werke in 20 Bänden*. Vol. 3, *Phänomenologie des Geistes*. Frankfurt am Main: Suhrkamp, 1970. Translated by A.V. Miller as *Phenomenology of Spirit*. Oxford: Oxford University Press, 1977.

Heidegger, Martin. *Hegel's Phänomenologie des Geistes*. Frankfurt am Main: Klostermann, 1980. Translated by Parvis Emad and Kenneth Maly as *Hegel's Phenomenology of Spirit*. Bloomington: Indiana University Press, 1988.

–. *Identity and Difference*. Bilingual edition. Translated by Joan Stambaugh. New York: Doubleday, 1961.

–. *The Question Concerning Technology and Other Essays*. Translated by William Lovitt. New York: Harper & Row, 1977.

–. *Sein und Zeit*. Tubingen: Niemeyer, 1979. Translated by John Macquarrie and Edward Robinson as *Being and Time*. New York: Harper & Row, 1962.

Lacoue-Labarthe, Philippe. *La Fiction du politique: Heidegger, l'art et la politique*. Paris: Christian Bourgois Editeur, 1987. Translated by Chris Turner as *Heidegger, Art and Politics: The Fiction of the Political*. Oxford: Basil Blackwell, 1990.

Plotnitsky, Arkady. "Closing the Eye: Hegel, Derrida and the Enclosure of Metaphysics", in *Agonistics: Arenas of Creative Contest*, ed. Janet Langstrum and Elizabeth Sauer. Albany, NY: SUNY Press, 1996.

–. *Complementarity: Anti-Epistemoloy After Bohr and Derrida*. Durham, NC: Duke University Press, 1994.

–. "History as Complementarity". In *Intersections between Nineteen-Century Philosophy and Contemporary Theory*, ed. David L. Clark and Tilottama Rajan. Albany, NY: SUNY Press, 1994.

–. "Re-: Reflecting, Re-membering, Re-collecting, ... Re-iterating, Re-etceterating (in) Hegel", *Postmodern Culture* (Summer 1995).

–. "Reading Hyppolite with Hegel". Foreword to Jean Hyppolite. *Introduction to Hegel's Philosophy of History*. Gainesville, Fl.: University Press of Florida, 1997.

–. *Reconfigurations: Critical Theory and General Economy*. Gainesville: University Press of Florida, 1993.

–. *In the Shadow of Hegel: Complementarity. History and the Unconscious*. Gainesville: University Press of Florida, 1993.

Stiegler, Bernard. "Persephone, Oedipus, Epimetheus". *Technema* 3 (Spring 1996), 97–112.

Chapter 7

Derrida and Science

Christopher Johnson

A significant feature of the phenomenon of structuralism, as it developed in France in the 1950s and 1960s, was its appeal to contemporary science. The loose confederation of disciplines designated as the "sciences humaines", and at their centre, anthropology, were in their different ways claimed to be sciences of the human. The structural anthropology of Lévi-Strauss itself claimed inspiration from the then recent theoretical advances of a number of scientific disciplines – biology, cybernetics, information theory – in addition to the fundamental contribution of linguistics. However limited the substance of such claims might appear in retrospect, at least one effect of structuralism was to extend the field of interdisciplinary exchange beyond the traditional circle of humanistic disciplines. The response of philosophy to the structuralist phenomenon was by no means a uniform one, and the celebrated "debate" between existentialism and structuralism is but one aspect of the total picture. Whatever the complications of this context (already, the status of philosophy within the human sciences is an ambiguous one), Lévi-Strauss uses the example of Sartre to stigmatize a certain kind of philosophy which had failed to follow and think through the implications of modern science.[1]

The episode of structuralism is an essential preface to the question of Derrida and science, of Derrida's relation to science, as it is in this context that his first major works are published. While Derrida recognizes the important contribution of structuralism to a certain phase of French thought, he is also strongly critical of it, questioning not only its linguistic reductionism but more generally the discourse of the human sciences, a discourse insufficiently cognizant of its roots in a certain history of philosophy.[2] Derrida's critique of Lévi-Strauss and the scientistic claims of structuralism is not, however, equivalent to a rejection of science itself, of (for example) a science that does not think. There is clear evidence in Derrida's work of a consistent interest in and attention to contemporary science, from his earliest to his more recent texts. This is especially discernible in the texts concerned with the concept of writing. As Derrida notes in *Of Grammatology*, there has been a conceptual transition, an epistemic shift within the structural-linguistic paradigm, involving a change in emphasis from the general idea of "language" to the more specific notion of "writing". This new questioning concerning writing comes partly from within philosophy itself, but it is also part of a wider scientific context with which philosophy has to reckon: "the contemporary biologist speaks of writing and program in relation to the most elementary processes of information within the living cell. And finally, whether it has essential limits or not, the entire field covered by the cybernetic program would be the field of writing".[3] The philosophical project which Derrida undertakes in *Of Grammatology* and related texts therefore cannot be abstracted from the context of what were at the time still recent developments in science.

Of course, the sciences Derrida is referring to here are not all of the sciences. Biology and cybernetics occupy what might be termed the "soft" end of the so-called "hard" sciences, and are of interest to philosophy and the human sciences precisely because they touch more immediately upon questions concerning the "human". The preoccupation of cybernetics with information transfer and automobile processes (communication and control) in animals, machines and humans offers to philosophical reflection new ways of thinking the relationship between the animal and the human, the human and the technological. The latter question, the question concerning technology, also reminds us that Derrida's own thinking on writing is not only inspired by scientific theory (it is precisely the traditional oppositions of "theory" and "practice", of "pure" and "applied" science which are in question here) but also, inseparably, by the practice of the new information and communication technologies developed in the post-war period. According to Jean-Joseph Goux, among other historical factors it is the presence of this new ambient technology which has made possible the grammatological inquiry.[4] Derrida's diagnosis of a certain "end" of (logocentric) metaphysics, of which the grammatological turn is a symptom, could therefore be seen as part of the total social fact of this qualititative as well as quantitative evolution of Western technological culture.

However, the incidence of the cybernetic-informational paradigm in Derrida's work should not be reduced simply to an enabling context, a mere element of "inspiration" or "influence". It should be remembered that the critique of logocentrism undertaken in *Of Grammatology* and adjacent texts is not limited to a simple overturning of the historical repression and reduction of writing in Western philosophy, and that parallel to this first moment of deconstruction is the formulation of a general theory of writing which is in many ways close to the cybernetic understanding of information in complex systems. In a manner typical of Derrida's style of thinking, this concept or theory or model of writing is not given any systematic definition or explication, but rather emerges from a process of dialogue with different thinkers or "moments" of the Western philosophical tradition, a dialogue extending across a number of different texts. Despite this dispersal or dissemination of Derrida's thinking on writing, one text in particular seems to condense a number of ideas central to cybernetic and informational science. This is the important essay on Freud published in 1967, "Freud and the Scene of Writing".[5]

Derrida's stated intention in "The Scene of Writing" is to follow the metaphor of writing as it is used in Freud's descriptions of the psychical apparatus, from his earliest works onwards. While the Freudian concepts of writing and trace are on the one hand limited by their entrenchment in a given history of positivistic and metaphysical thought, on the other hand Derrida indicates Freud's critical and careful handling of such concepts, the conscious nominalism of his hypothetical constructions. Freud's use of the graphical metaphor is therefore not simple, it is not reducible to the merely illustrative or didactic use of the metaphor found in traditional philosophical descriptions of the relationship between reason and experience, perception and memory. The first phase of Derrida's reading of Freud concentrates not on the scriptural metaphor itself but on the memory trace or, to use Freud's term, the facilitation (*Bahnung*). He shows how Freud's model of the facilitation and of the psychical apparatus radicalizes conventional empiricist and substantialist conceptions of psychological processes such as perception and memory. First, he questions the concept of facilitation as a present, empirical substance. Though Freud wishes to retain the idea of facilitation as simple quantity, opposing a transparent quality of consciousness to an opaque quantity of memory, the concept itself is resistant to such reduction. Rather, Freud's own speculation on the process of memory shows it to reside in the differences or relations between facilitations rather than in their individual substance.[6] Inseparable from this differential conception of the facilitation is its non-present and non-simultaneous temporality. For Freud, one of the important functions of the network of facilitations is to permit otherwise fatal quantities of excitation external to the organism to be meted out and stored, that is, distributed in space. Equally important, however, is the distribution of excitations in discrete repetitions, or periodic differenes. Derrida assimilates this notion of adjournment through distribution, of temporal as well as spatial difference (interval and repetition), with his own concept of *différance*.[7] Finally, the facilitation is located in a system which itself is not a simple and homogenous space. The psychical apparatus, as Freud describes it, is a stratified system, a collection or consecution of systems, instances or agencies. This complication or co-implication of instances virtualizes psychical space and makes it irreducible to purely empirical observation or description. It could be said that with such a complication of space, there is no determinable first or last instance.[8]

Derrida's problematization of the substance, temporality and spatial location of the memory trace in Freud, while owing something to previous philosophies of difference (Hegel, Nietzsche, Heidegger), is also clearly influenced by contemporary information science. His construction, with and through Freud, of a dynamic model of the psychical apparatus as a differential, discontinuous and complex (stratified, multi-levelled) system is in many ways similar to the models of cybernetic and information theory. This similarity is pointed out by Wilden, who compares Derrida's reading of difference in Freud with Bateson's conception of information as difference.[9] According to Bateson, what is important is not so much the quantities of energy or substance supporting the transmission of information, as the differences that the information represents. Wilden quotes Buckley:

> Though "information" is dependent upon some physical base or energy flow, the energy component is entirely subordinate to the particular form or structure of variations that the physical base or flow may manifest ... This structured variation – the marks of writing, the sounds of speech, the molecular arrangement of the genetic code of DNA, etc. – is still only raw material or energy unless it "corresponds" to, or matches in some important way, the structure of variations of other components to which it may thereby become dynamically related.[10]

Bateson's own definition of information adds to this structural description the temporal dimension of derferment, and again can be compared with Derrida's notion of *différance*: "The technical term 'information' may be succinctly defined as any difference which makes a difference in some later event. This definition is fundamental for all analysis of cybernetic systems and organization".[11]

Derrida's reading of Freud, like Wilden's, therefore situates Freud between two paradigms: the thermodynamic paradigm of the late nineteenth and early twentieth centuries, concerned with forces, quantities and substances, and the informational paradigm of the present period, which deals with differences, forms and relations. While many critics of Freud point to the weakness of his bioenergetic and deterministic explanations of mental processes, Wilden and Derrida show how this traditional substantialist-materialist perspective is in Freud's text also coupled with a semiotic understanding of such processes.

Derrida's mediation of Freud in "The Scene of Writing" is not, however, restricted to the aforementioned conceptual parallels with modern science; as was noted above, the theoretical advances in the informational and cybernetic sciences in the post-war period are also, irreducibly, technological advances. In Derrida's essay on Freud the question of technology becomes increasingly central as he explores how Freud's early neurological and anatomical descriptions of psychical processes are superseded by speculation of a more metaphorical kind, more precisely by speculation involving the use of scriptural metaphors. This metaphor of writing becomes a working model when it is combined with the machine in the example of the Mystic Writing Pad. The Mystic Pad, with its ingenious laminated structure, is superior to Freud's previous models in that it accounts for the dual capacity of the psychical apparatus for both retention and infinite reception of stimuli, the mental functions of perception and memory which Freud believed to be mutually exclusive. It is easy to understand Derrida's interest in Freud's model. With its combination of system and writing, machine and code, it is an infinitely more sophisticated simulation of psychical processes than the traditional metaphors of soul or psyche as inscribed wax tablet. As a complex system of inscription it integrates the different aspects of facilitation and psychical apparatus explained above: ephemerality and discontinuity, stratification and non-simultaneity.

Typically, however, Derrida is not content to indicate the heuristic advantages of Freud's model, and this is where he parts company with Freud. Freud's use of the analogy of the Mystic Pad is in the final instance a purely instrumental one; like the Lévi-Straussian bricoleur, he adopts the model insofar as it is approximate to the object he wishes to describe, but discards it when it no longer serves that purpose. Freud concedes that the model of the Mystic Pad fails to imitate the actual operation of human memory to the extent that it does not possess the autonomy of the human psychical apparatus, that is, it does not dispose of and use the capacity of cathexis. It is at this point, as Freud articulates the limits of his analogy, that Derrida questions this limitation. Despite the sophistication of Freud's model, his final distinction between the living human psyche and the dead technology of the Mystic Pad rejoins the traditional philosophical conception of technology as external supplement, an auxiliary but not essential part of the human.[12] For his part, Derrida suggests that Freud has not completely followed through the implications of his own thought. The very possibility of the metaphorical passage between psyche and model – their resemblance – would indicate a more fundamental kind of relationship between the two. The very possibility of the supplementation of consciousness, the very necessity of its externalization, would indicate a certain "death" at the heart of this consciousness. As in a cybernetic circuit, the externalization of the "human" would also be internalization of the "non-human", a reciprocal process of affection and modification.

As can be seen, Derrida's dialogue with Freud is also a dialogue with contemporary science, or more specifically the branch of modern science concerned with complex systems. Whereas Freud follows traditional closed-system scientific practice in his separation of psyche and world, the human and the technical, the essential and the auxiliary, Derrida refuses such punctuation of context, and extends Freud's internal stratification of instances into the external space of the world: "The subject of writing is a system of relations between strata: the Mystic Pad, the psyche, society, the world".[13] This systemic conception of the psyche is very close to Bateson's notion of mind: "the mental world – the mind – the world of information processing – is not limited by the skin".[14] It describes a system in interaction with its context rather than the isolated entities and processes of classical science. It is also part of a historical context in which modern simulations of vital and human processes, infinitely more sophisticated than Freud's humble artefact, are increasingly calling into question the traditional line of demarcation between the natural and the artificial.[15]

The model of writing which emerges from Derrida's dialogue with Freud in "The Scene of Writing" and texts contemporary to it can be seen as being constructed around a complex of terms: inscription, difference, archi-writing, trace, deferment (*différance*). So far we have examined its possible relations with one of the two sciences Derrida mentions as being of special relevance to the grammatological enquiry, cybernetics. The other science he mentions is biology. If Derrida's conception of writing questions the conventional distinction between the human and the technical, it also questions the traditional definition of the human as "life", as the "living" – *le vivant*. As biologist François Jacob points out, the discoveries of genetic science in the 1950s and 1960s were very much dependent on linguistic models, more specifically on the metaphor of the genetic code as a kind of script.[16] For the most part, Derrida's engagement with genetic science is not a direct one. Instead, it could be said that his reflection on writing is extended into the realm of the biological by a process of rhetorical accretion, perceptible at the level of what could be termed his "bio-genetic" metaphors. The systematic use of such metaphors is first apparent in *Dissemination*, and the complex of associations built up in that text is extended and developed in a number of subsequent texts, most notably *Glas* and *The Post Card*. The conceptual matrix of writing–trace–difference–*différance*, characteristic of Derrida's initial philosophy of inscription, is thus supplemented by the bio-genetic figures of dissemination–germ(ination)–seminal *différance*. This supplement is also an inflection: while in *Of Grammatology*, for example, the concept of writing is already being thought conjointly with the question of life, it is only with the elaboration of the later, bio-genetic lexicon that Derrida begins to explore in an overtly rhetorical manner the questions of life and writing.

It is only possible here to reconstruct part of Derrida's dialogue – his lateral dialogue – with genetic science. Again, this takes place in the context of a continued interrogation of Western metaphysics, of its representation of life or the principle of life in the concept of the seed or germ. This concept, Derrida tells us in *Glas*, is a key component of Hegel's speculative dialectic, figuratively linking the different orders he describes. The seed which anticipates (for example) the tree, and which is also its end, is an ideal figuration of the reappropriating return of mind to itself after its passage through nature or Experience. During this circular journey, nothing is lost, all contradictions along the way are resumed in the ascendent work of the *Aufhebung*. In its Hegelian incarnation, the seed is therefore a closed monad, containing and mirroring in their virtuality all subsequent contingencies in the development of the system. This reappropriating return of seed to seed, the satisfaction of the accomplishment of Absolute Mind is also patrilinear, it is the self-inseminating spirit of God the Father, which does not tolerate sexual difference.[17]

Derrida's displacement or deconstruction of Hegel's representation of the seed takes place firstly by a process of pluralization: what he proposes is not the serene unfolding of a singular germ or seed, but the plural scattering of dissemination, such as that described in his discourse on flowers in the right-hand column of *Glas*. As he had already asserted in *Dissemination*, where the concept is first introduced: "There is no first insemination. The semen is already swarming. The 'primal' insemination is dissemination".[18] In Derrida's text, therefore, the germ, far from being the *arche* and the *eschaton* of a given system, becomes the principle of dispersal and of random combination. This movement of dissemination, or germination, as it is sometimes called, has no predetermined pathway, its *telos* is indeterminate; in contrast with the ascent of the Hegelian system towards the Absolute, dissemination descends, and descends catastrophically. Unlike the stately return to the self-same implied in idealist teleology (a single line of descent, a male economy), Derridean dissemination is a continuous drift of differences which has no origin and knows of no determinate future. The system is not pulled into the future by a mysterious first (and last) principle, but is pushed a tergo by what is handed down, selected and recombined, from its ancestral past. This philosophy is, in essence, a philosophy of evolution.

On the one hand, Derrida's elaborate juxtaposition in *Glas* of alternative readings of the germ is clearly a staging of two different traditions in Western metaphysics, materialism and idealism. His privileging of the materialist tradition is visible in his inflection of the word towards an "atomistic" interpretation, where the germ is not the self-contained, self-reproducing entity of idealist philosophy, but a fissiparous and proliferating particle which exists only in combination with other particles, like the Lucretian atom. On the other hand, and inseparable from this reactivation of atomist physics, Derrida's germ is an interpellation of contemporary genetic science. This can be seen in his insistence on the isomorphism between atom, term and germ, which evokes the modern understanding of the molecular and informational basis of heredity. This does not mean a static combination of elements – atom, term or germ –, subject to a single code. In Lucretius, the dynamic principle preceding combination and which persists as a perturbing force within the constituted system is the clinamen. Like Derrida's trace, the clinamen is not a thing or an object, it is, properly speaking, nothing. More precisely, it is a movement, or an atom of movement (but not an atom), and is itself imperceptible. In Derridean terms, it might be described as pure spacing. As the indeterminate principle of the code, it is itself not part of the code, what Derrida refers to in *Dissemination* as the supplement to the code:

> As the heterogeneity and absolute exteriority of the seed, seminal [*différance*] does constitute itself into a program, but it is a program that cannot be formalized. For reasons that can be formalized. The infinity of its code, its rift, then, does not take a form saturated with self-presence in the

encyclopedic circle. It is attached, so to speak, to the incessant falling of a supplement to the code.[19]

In temporal terms, the code, as Derrida understands it, is therefore constituted in process rather than in anticipation. Despite the suggestion of precedence implied in the articulation of the word "pro-gramme", the germ, the gram, the trace are never absolutely primary. There is instead a kind of precipitation towards sense that is ignorant of its future. All this is very close to the biological understanding of the genetic code, which is metamorphic, constantly subject to the destabilizing effects of mutation. The process of evolution (the context of the code) is not an ascent of species towards some determinate apex of development, but the selection after the event of mutations most amenable to environmental constraints. By virtue of a feedback process – both positive and negative – the genetic code is therefore regulating (before) but also regulated (after) in the sense that its pro-gramme is executed in a context that is perpetually changing, hence perpetually modifying the conditions of possibility of the code. The supplement to the code described above is this continual differing-from-itself of the code as it descends the evolutionary slope. Of course, the process of selection that operates a posteriori upon the code's unprogrammed drift gives the appearance of the necessity of the forms it produces. Like all auto-mobile processes, it has something of the uncanny about it, and is therefore, in the idealist interpretation, attributed to a transcendent (anthropologized) instance of intentionality, that is, given a theological and teleological explanation. According to a certain materialist tradition, on the other hand, the *unheimlich* is quite *heimisch*, it is already quite at home within the system.

Survival – biological survival – is dependent on this double bind of chance and necessity, that is, the conservatism of the genetic code, the strict execution of its content (without which there would be nothing) and the perturbation of its supplement (without which there would be no change). It would be a mistake, however, to interpret Derrida's interpellation of genetic science as proposing an a priority of the biological. His inflection of the seed metaphor, via the atomist tradition, clearly does not essentialize life or vitalize phenomena. Such essentializing is in fact more typical of the idealist and logocentric tradition, which is predicated on the closed economy of what is proper to the human, to life, to consciousness. The atomist tradition, by contrast, necessarily sees a certain continuity between nature, the human and culture. One important consequence of the materialist premise that atoms are not endowed with intelligence or life, is that life itself is viewed as merely a property of organized matter. In their turn, the many possible extensions of life – the technology of writing for example – are similarly organized, that is, they depend upon a syntax of combination. At the basis of "life", therefore, there is a certain death, or non-being, continued into "life" through its extensions or articulations, and necessary to it.

When, therefore, Derrida aphoristically proposes that "each term is indeed a germ, and each germ a term",[20] he is not simply proposing an appropriate, but ultimately arbitrary, metaphor. The metaphor of writing, as it is articulated with the genetic and the biological in Derrida's texts, is not simply metaphor. One could attempt here to employ a more discriminating vocabulary, to speak of isomorphism rather than metaphor. But even this is not a sufficient approximation to what

Derrida is arguing, it merely displaces the problem, which is that the similarity of form (isomorphism) of writing and genetic code is indicative of their identity. Quite literally, the term is a germ and the germ is a term. Viewed from within the context of evolution, which is a continuum, they are the same thing. Functionally, there is a genetic or genealogical continuity between the two, an unbroken line of descent from the one to the other. Of course, formulated in this way, this genealogy would appear to be self-evident, but as Derrida's analyses of speech and writing show, the logocentric tradition has consistently denied and repressed such a continuity, drawing a limit to the "human" at the frontier of speech, as if speech were not also a (communication) technology. As is demonstrated in the impressive reasoning of *Of Grammatology* and other texts of the same period, speech is simply an instance of the generalized writing that is the structure of all systems. This general writing, like writing in the common sense of the word or, more precisely, of which writing is an extension, is the condition of possibility of the transmission of information (communication) within and between all complex systems. Without the trace, the consigning of information to a memory or archive, there is no communication.[21] The genetic code which ensures the invariant reproduction of species is just an example (though for "life" and the "human", the most important example) of such a writing.

It follows that Derrida's articulation of the biological and the textual ("the term is a germ") does not simply place writing proper in the wider, enveloping context of the genetic, but in turn presents the genetic as a subset or special case of the more abstract category of the trace. So the above formulation could be rephrased more clearly as "the term (scriptural) is a germ (genetic) is a term (trace)", which expresses an ascending order of generality. If the continuity of species taught by Darwinian science in the nineteenth century prompted many to ask, what is man?, the findings of genetics, cybernetics and information theory in this century inevitably lead to Schrödinger's question, what is life?

This displacement of the biogenetic is particularly well illustrated in Derrida's reading of Benjamin's reflections on translation. In *The Task of the Translator* Benjamin uses a series of familial, genealogical and genetic metaphors to describe the process of translation from one language to another, metaphors which are neither arbitrary nor innocent. The theory behind Benjamin's metaphorical correlation of the textual and the genetic, according to Derrida, is not simply that we as living beings produce texts, use them, translate the vital into the textual, but that the translation of a text in general is a more fundamental process than life itself. Derrida insists therefore that Benjamin's use of the metaphor of the maturation of a seed, when discussing the difficulties of translating Mallarmé (again, it is a question of the seed), is not vitalistic:

> The allusion to the maturation of a seed could resemble a vitalist or geneticist metaphor; it would come, then, in support of the genealogical and parental code which seems to dominate this text. In fact it seems necessary here to invert this order and recognize what I have elsewhere proposed to call the "metaphoric catastrophe": far from knowing first what "life" or "family" mean whenever we use these familiar values to talk about language and translation, it is rather starting from the notion of a language and its "survival" in translation that we could have access to the notion of what life and family mean.[22]

This "metaphoric catastrophe", first referred to in *The Post Card*,[23] is a restatement of the structure of inversion described above: not only is the term a germ, but the germ is, in the most general sense, a term. The continuous chain that extends from writing (technology) to the biological to evolution is a subset of the more general category of the trace. One arrives therefore at a non-biological theory of evolution in which the testamentary structure of survival (in the delegation and translation of the trace), the supplementary *Über-leben* over and above (before and after) the economy of life, is the organizing principle.

Derrida's commentary on Benjamin shows quite clearly that this metaphorical inversion, which is more than simply metaphorical, is consciously articulated in Benjamin's text: the fact that mind, history, art have a "life" of their own, survive over and above their biological support, leads us to think of natural life in terms of the wider life that is history, and not vice versa.[24] At the same time, Derrida extends this argument and pushes it to its logical limit, by proposing that it is the structure of translation, the structure of survival which is fundamental: "In this sense the surviving dimension is an a priori – and death would not change it at all".[25] Derrida is thus proposing, via Benjamin, a form of pure translation that is logically prior to the "original", a survival that is prior to "life".

If survival for any system is delegation in the trace, the consigning to a "memory" whose principles are more general than human or even biological (genetic) memory, this memory, which is the "history" of the system (or more exactly, its future, its future anterior), is therefore not a static script. In an "evolutionary" situation, reproduction is never reproduction of the same, which is ultimately counter-adaptive. Delegation is also translation. The Überleben is the supplementary Übersetzen described in Derrida's reading of Benjamin which displaces or transplants what it translates. Survival is only ensured by the alteration (translation) of the original, the differing from itself of the code (the supplement to the code), the perpetual rewriting of its history. If one follows the logic of Derrida's rhetorical play on the word "trace", then the anagram of trace/*écart* proposed in Dissemination gives a usefully condensed definition of this double-bound structure: the trace is both *reste* and *restance*, deposit and movement. Within this structure, the *écart* of the trace is more fundamental than its remainder, since it is only through such spacing that new structures and new possibilities are produced.

Derrida's insistence on the primacy of the *écart* within the trace (of survival over life, of translation over text) bears a striking resemblance to current scientific thinking on life processes. Whereas biologists have traditionally taken reproduction to be the defining feature of living systems, the category of fluctuation is now considered to be logically prior to that of reproduction. The biologist Henri Atlan, for example, takes issue with François Jacob's suggestion that the "dream" of the cell is to become two cells, arguing instead for the logical primacy of perturbation, of the departure from equilibrium (*écart d'équilibre*) over reproduction in biology.[26] This notion of perturbation is a common feature of what in systems theory are termed "ultrastable" or "multistable" systems, that is, systems having a number of possible stable states, made possible by the "looseness" or indeterminacy of their connections. Such systems are "equifinal" to the extent that while their ostensible aim is reproduction, there are a number of ways of achieving this aim. This potential for alternative pathways of development can, by a process of feedback with a changing environment, actually change the structure or programme of the system. Because the code changes while attempting to remain the same, reproduction will tend in each instance to be the replication of the same but different. Hence similar initial conditions may lead to dissimilar end-states. This process of divergence, or "multifinality", is not amenable to deterministic or even statistical calculation, its direction is not predictable in the same way that the development of a less complex (closed) system is predictable. Evolution is one example of a multifinal process.

As can be seen, there are a number of significant correspondences between Derrida's philosophy of writing and the concepts of systems theory. The systems concepts of ultrastability, equifinality and multifinality might be usefully compared with the key notions of play and dissemination in Derrida's work. His extended speculation on the figure of the letter in *The Post Card*, for example, combines all of these motifs – scriptural, communicational, systemic and biological – in its questioning of the concept of a rigid law of destination. It is precisely the play of destination (the possibility of perturbation, noise, random fluctuation) which makes the system work, whereas perfect transmission, perfect reproduction, would signify literally the death of the system, paralysing its potential for change. To paraphrase Derrida's remark, quoted earlier: the law (of destination) cannot be formalized for reasons that can be formalized. Or put another way, the law of destination is a law of destabilization, as Derrida argues in *My Chances*:

> Language, however, is only one among those systems of marks that claim this curious tendency as their property: they simultaneously incline towards increasing the reserves of random indetermination as well as the capacity for coding and overcoding or, in other words, for control and self-regulation. Such competition between randomness and code disrupts the very systematicity of the system while it also, however, regulates the restless, unstable interplay of the system. Whatever its singularity in this respect, the linguistic system of these traces or marks would merely be, it seems to me, just a particular example of the law of destabilization.[27]

Again, language, as a form of writing, as a system of marks, is for Derrida only an example of the class of complex, ultrastable systems which combine chance and necessity, coding and redundancy. It is in passages such as this that one can see the extent to which Derrida's thinking on system and writing has, over the years, developed in interaction with some of the more interesting aspects of modern scientific thought. If, as we have seen, his earlier thinking on writing and trace recognizes the importance of developments in cybernetics and biology, his later work seems increasingly to gesture towards their generalization in the concepts of systems theory.

The preceding analysis has attempted to show some of the ways in which Derrida's work reflects or mediates aspects of contemporary science. It deals of course with only one dimension of his work, but it does show a thinker open to the implications of science, of what science gives us to think. At the same time, as a philosopher, Derrida's relation to what I have perhaps too unproblematically referred to as "science" is more complex. If the body of knowledge known as "systems theory", for example, rejects the closed-system epistemology of traditional science in favour of an ecology of implicated systems, it could be argued that in its discursive practice and with respect to the phenomena it treats, it is still – necessarily – restricted to the subject-object dichotomies of traditional science. In a sense, for scientific discourse, this is the final frontier which cannot be crossed, only probed. In a number of his texts, however, Derrida initiates a step beyond this frontier by taking the notion of the open system to its logical limit, including his own discourse as an example, and more than an example, of the systems he describes. This kind of self-reference is arguably only possible from a position outside of science. It represents the critical mission of a philosophy which questions conventional framings of systems and punctuations of context, asking questions which science itself finally cannot ask if it is to function without aporia as science.

University of Keele, UK

Notes

[1] See for instance Lévi-Strauss's remarks on Sartre in Didier Eribon, *Conversations with Claude Lévi-Strauss*, translated by Paula Wissing (Chicago: University of Chicago Press, 1991), pp. 118–19.

[2] "Structure, Sign and Play in the Discourse of the Human Sciences", in *Writing and Difference*, translated by Alan Bass (London: Routledge, 1978), pp. 284–5.

[3] *Of Grammatology*, translated by Gayatri Chakravorty Spivak (Baltimore and London: Johns Hopkins University Press, 1976), p. 9.

[4] "Du graphème au chromosome", *Les lettres françaises* 1429 (29 March 1972), 7.

[5] *Writing and Difference*, pp. 196–231.

[6] Ibid., pp. 201, 204.

[7] Ibid., p. 202.

[8] Ibid., pp. 215–16.

[9] Anthony Wilden, *System and Structure. Essays in Communication and Exchange* (London: Tavistock Publications, 1980), p. 398.

[10] Ibid., p. 138.

[11] Gregory Bateson, *Steps to an Ecology of Mind* (New York: Ballantine Books, 1972), p. 381.

[12] *Writing and Difference*, p. 227.

[13] Ibid., p. 227.

[14] *Steps to an Ecology of Mind*, p. 454.

[15] *Writing and Difference*, p. 228.

[16] "Le modèle linguistique en biologie", *Critique* 322 (March 1974), 195–205.

[17] *Glas*, translated by John P. Leavey Jr and Richard Rand (Lincoln and London: University of Nebraska Press, 1984), pp. 27–31a; 116a.

[18] *Dissemination*, translated by Barbara Johnson (Chicago: University of Chicago Press, 1981), p. 304.

[19] Ibid., p. 52.

[20] Ibid., p. 304.

[21] See Wilden, *System and Structure*, pp. 374, 446.

[22] "Des Tours de Babel", translated by Joseph F. Graham, in *Difference in Translation*, edited by Joseph F. Graham (Ithaca and London: Cornell University Press, 1985), p. 178.

[23] *The Post Card. From Socrates to Freud and Beyond*, translated by Alan Bass (Chicago and London: University of Chicago Press, 1987), p. 46.

[24] "Des Tours de Babel", pp. 178–9.
[25] Ibid., p. 182.
[26] Henri Atlan, *L'organisation biologique et la théorie de l'information* (Paris: Hermann, 1972), p. 224.
[27] "My Chances/Mes Chances: A Rendezvous with some Epicurean Stereophonies", translated by Irene Harvey and Avital Ronell, in *Taking Chances: Derrida, Psychoanalysis and Literature*, edited by Joseph H. Smith and William Kerrigan (Baltimore and London: Johns Hopkins University Press, 1984), pp. 2–3.

Chapter 8

As if it were Possible, "within such limits" ...

Jacques Derrida

Despite the delay of what begins here, this won't, as one might suspect, be about the last word. A reader must, especially, not expect any last word. It is excluded, nearly impossible, that for my part I dare to lay claim to one. It would even be necessary, another protocol of the contract, *not to* lay claim to one or expect one.

Perhaps, the Im-Possible (Aphoristic I)

I no longer know how the declaration I've just risked in ordinary language can be read. A sign of modesty or an expression of presumption? "Does he mean, modestly, perhaps with affected timidity, that he will be unable to propose, by way of an answer, anything at all that is sure and definitive, not even the least *last word*?" a reader might wonder. "Would he have the arrogance to suggest that he still has so many answers in reserve after what would be, in sum, in place and on behalf of a *last word*, a simple *forward*?" another would add. "But then, how to interpret the possibility of these two interpretations of the *last word*?" a third would sigh. Then the fourth, sententiously: "Have you read Austin on "*the crux of the Last Word*?", with respect to ordinary language, in *A Plea for Excuses*? Or – three times – Blanchot,[1] in *Le dernier mot, Le tout dernier mot, Le dernier mot*, namely on a certain *il y a* which is going to resemble the one of Levinas and which one can absolutely not, in irreducible ordinary language, translate without remainder? Especially not as "*there is*" or "*Es gibt*"?

Will I dare to add my voice to this concert of hypotheses and virtual utterances? Perhaps, then, I would orient things differently. For example towards an irreducible modality of "perhaps". That would make any authority of the "*last word*" tremble. Haven't I tried elsewhere[2] to analyze at once the possibility and the necessity of this "perhaps?", its promise and fatality, its implication in all experience, at the approach of *that* which comes (ce *qui vient*), (this) (other) *who* comes ([*ce*] [*l'autre*] *qui vient*) from the future and gives place to what is called an event? But this experience of "perhaps" would be *at once* that of the possible *and* the impossible, of the possible *as* impossible. If only that which is already possible happens, therefore anticipated and expected, it doesn't make an event. The event is only possible when it comes from the impossible. It happens as the coming of the impossible, there where a "perhaps" (*peut-être*) deprives us of all assurance and leaves the future to the future. This "perhaps" is necessarily allied to a "yes": yes, yes to what (who) comes ([*ce*] *qui vient*). This "yes" would be common to the affirmation and the answer, it would even come before any question. A *peut-être* like "perhaps"[3] (it may happen),[4] one would say, rather than the insubstantial *"vielleicht,"* rather than the call to being or the ontological insinuation, the *to be or not to be*[5] of a *maybe*, is perhaps that which, exposed like the "yes" to the event, that is to say to the experience of what arrives (happens)[6] and of *who* then arrives (de *qui* alors arrive), far from interrupting the question, gives it its breath. How is one to keep from ever giving up the question – its urgency or its interminable necessity – without also making the question, even less than the answer, into a "last word?" This is close to my heart and mind, but perhaps this is no longer a question or an answer. Perhaps it is something else entirely, we'll have to get to it. The "perhaps" keeps the question alive, and assures, perhaps, its sur-vival (*sur-vie*). What does a "perhaps" mean, then, at the disarticulated juncture of the possible and the impossible, of the possible *as* impossible?

Of Ordinary Language: Excuses (Aphoristic II)

I've taken too long to respond to the studies we've just read, as the authors know. Is this forgivable?

But I ask forgiveness for it. Sincerely. But not without engaging myself once more in a response. Thus I promise to *do* something, which is called "responding," and to *do* it as it is believed a response should always be done: by *speaking*. Not by joining the gesture to the speech, as it is said in ordinary language, but *by doing* something *with words*, according to Austin's formula. Why name here the well-known inventor of a now familiar distinction? Although the pair of concepts performative–constative has a somewhat recent origin, it has become canonical. Despite its author's amused stubbornness in only following "ordinary language," this pair has changed a great many things in the less ordinary language of philosophy and theory in this century. But – first paradox – this is a distinction in whose purity Austin himself has often said he doesn't believe.[7] He even declared it at the moment of giving a talk, irrefutable in my eyes, on ordinary language and precisely, as is the case with me here, on the subject of the excuse and forgiveness: "Certainly, then, ordinary language is not the last word (words which he had written a little earlier, not without irony, but as a quote of ordinary language, in capital letters: 'Then, for the Last Word'); in principle it can everywhere but supplemented and improved upon and superseded. Only remember, it [ordinary language] is the first *word*."[8]

At this point, at this allusion to the "first *word*", Austin adds a footnote. One recognizes the singularity and the efficacity of his philosophical style: "And forget, for once and for a while, that other curious question 'Is it true?' May we?" I thought, for a moment, as a manner of excuse and by way of an answer to all the magnificent texts I've been given to read here, of proposing a sort of interpretation or "close reading"[9] of "A Plea for Excuses."

I won't do it. But "for once and for a while": what modesty! what cunning! what wisdom! "For a while",[10] this means "for the moment", a rather brief moment, sometimes "a pretty long time," or even "a very long time", perhaps forever, but not necessarily once and for all. For how much time, then? Perhaps the time of a talk or an article, for example an article on the excuse and forgiveness, "A Plea for

Excuses". Without asking forgiveness and without making excuses, without doing it explicitly, but nonetheless without forgetting to apologize for it, Austin begins his article by announcing with irony that he is not going to treat his subject. He's not going to answer the question, and what he's going to say will not correspond to the subject as it has been announced: *Excuses*. Perhaps he is going to *respond* to his readers and his listeners, since he's addressing them, but perhaps without answering the question, their questions, or their expectations. First sentence: "The subject of this paper, Excuses, is one not to be treated, but only to be introduced, within such limits." He excuses himself, then, for not seriously treating the excuse and for remaining, and leaving his audience, in ignorance on the subject of what *to excuse* means. And this at the moment when (performative contradiction?) he begins by excusing himself – by pretending to do it, rather, by excusing himself for not treating the subject of the excuse. Will he treat it? Perhaps. It is for the reader to judge, for the addressee to decide. It's like a postcard whose virtual addressee will have to decide whether or not he will receive it and whether it's indeed to him that it's addressed. The signature is left to the initiative, the responsibility, to the discretion of the other. Let's get to work. One will sign, if one signs, at the moment of arriving at the destination, not at the origin. (As for the hypothesis according to which Austin would have allowed himself – himself also, himself already – to be caught in a "performative contradiction", of which we wouldn't have even formed a suspicion without him, let us smile at this idea along with the specter of Austin.) As if it were possible to escape each performative contradiction! And as if it were possible to exclude the idea that Austin would have played at illustrating this inevitable trap!

Would a great traditional philosopher have dared to do this? Can one imagine Kant or Hegel admitting that he won't treat the proposed subject? Can one see them excusing themselves for not doing justice to the excuse, to the subject or the proposed title, "A Plea for Excuses" "within such limits"?

"A Plea for Excuses" may always (perhaps) have been nothing but the title naming the one singular gesture of Austin that day, or the show, in a word, that he, and no other, puts on, when he asks to be excused for not treating the subject. A title is always a noun. Here, the referent of this name is what Austin does (he asks for excuses) and not what he's treating, since he excuses himself for not treating it. Perhaps all he did was to introduce the subject by giving an example – his – which is this: precisely that he excuses himself for not treating the subject. But as soon as he gives the introduction, he knows what he should talk about, and thus what he's started to talk about it, even as he says he's incapable of doing it "within such limits". I would quite like to take him as a model, that is to say as an example, or as a pretext – or as an excuse. Let's remember Rousseau, who confesses, concerning the famous episode of the stolen ribbon in his *Confessions* (Book II), "I excused myself upon the first thing that offered itself".

To Respond – Analogies (Aphoristic III)

In any case, if one responded without failing the other; if one responded precisely, fully, adequately; if one adjusted the response perfectly to fit the question, the demand and the expectation, would one still be responding? Would something happen? Would an event occur? Or just the accomplishment of a program, a calculable operation? To be worthy of this name, must a response not *surprise* by some disruptive novelty? And thus by an anachronic disadjustment? Mustn't it respond "beside the point", (*à côté de la question*) in sum? *Precisely and just* beside the point? Not just anywhere, or anyhow, or anything, but *precisely and just* beside the point – but at the very moment that the question is doing everything to address itself to the other, truly, to the expectation of the other, in consensually defined conditions (contract, rules, norms, concepts, language, code, and so on) and with *directness* (*droiture*) itself? These two conditions of the question appear incompatible, but each is as incontestable, it seems to me, as the other. Here, perhaps, is the impasse in which I find myself – in which I find myself paralyzed. Here is the aporia where I've put myself. I find myself put here, in truth, even before establishing myself here.

If I could treat my subject and respond to so many virtual questions, I would perhaps be tempted to *retranslate*, at great risk, all the problematics so forcefully elaborated in the essays that precede me here. I would be tempted to *reformulate* them in the big question of ordinary language. To take just two examples, in the direction of the fine analyses of John Sallis and Karel Thein, who help us rethink – differently but with equal amounts of force and necessity – our philosophical memory, where it is indebted to the Greek idiom: where is the border, within a language that is called natural, thus not totally formalizable, between ordinary usage and philosophical usage? How does one do it, for example, when one uses, in everyday life in Greece, but also, from the moment of Plato's work on, words like *pharmakon* (poison and/or remedy, sometimes undecidably) or *khora* (ordinary place, locality, village), versus the unique *khora* of the *Timaeus* which, despite so many appearances, no longer has any relation, even by *analogy*, to the other. (This question of the analogy awaits us precisely in the place that Thein speaks of the "limits of the analogy"; I'll have to come back to it, because it will undoubtedly govern all of my remarks; it will provide me with the most general form of my address to the authors of the articles collected here.) In a word, which won't be the last: how – according to what economy, what transaction – to treat the analogy, both the analogy between relations of analogy and the analogy between relations of heterology, *between* the maintenance and the rupture of the analogy? Is the first analogy possible or impossible, legitimate or abusive? How to explain that the relation *(logos)* of analogy is named by one of the terms of proportionality, for example between *logos* and soul, *pharmakon* and body? This question is remarkably elaborated by Thein. It will traverse the entire discussion, more or less visibly. An analogous question seems to present itself on the subject of the different uses of the word *khora*, in daily life and in philosophical discourse, but also in philosophical contexts (such as the *Republic* and the *Timaeus*) both common and heterogeneous. These contexts seem to have between them relations of articulable analogy *and* of irreducible dissociation, one could say aphoristic or diaphoristic; they stay radically untranslatable from one to the other, at least if one believes in the stability of what is called here a discursive context. In particular, in certain passages discovered and rigorously analyzed by Sallis, when the word *khora* seems to have a different meaning from the one it has in the *Timaeus* (without relation to the good and the *epekeina tes ousias*), and thus designates the place of the sun itself, "where the good and the *khora* are brought into a very remarkable proximity".

And here already, caught in the ordinary language of various natural languages, is the syntax of a first question, of a first problem. It is the problem that is a priori supplementary to a complement. To the complement of a word in the language which is a verb: *to respond*, yes, it should be done, here now. Yes, one could attempt it, be tempted to attempt it, certainly, but to respond to *whom*? *before whom*? *about what*? and *what*? As for "responding", for the grammar of the verb and the pragmatism of the act, we must acknowledge *four complements and four syntaxes*.

The first possible answer, perhaps, on the subject of the response, and first concerning the *first two complements* (*to whom*? *before whom*?): to respond *to* whoever, thus, and *before* whoever has at least *read* – this is the first condition – *read*, and of course understood, analyzed, or even written the texts that precede my own here – that is to say some earlier works that they discuss themselves, for example, those of the great canonical tradition, from Plato and Aristotle to Kant, Hegel, Husserl or Heidegger, and so on, in their relation to science, but also the works that descend from these today more or less legitimately and in a minor key, including my own, hypothetically: all of us here are bound by the contract which the director of the Revue Internationale de Philosophie proposed to us. Each reader is supposed to accept such a contract, as are those whose names appear on the Contents page.

The second possible response, perhaps, on the subject of the response, the one I believe I'll have to choose in any case, but this time concerning the *last two complements* (*for what* and *what*): not answer *for* what I've written (can I myself answer in any reasonable way? don't they talk about it more clearly than I do?) but perhaps answer (and here is *what*) by saying a few words, within such limits, about the questions, difficulties, aporias, dead ends, I no longer dare say "problems", in the midst of which I'm presently struggling and which will no doubt trouble me for a long time. I will borrow (in order to beg forgiveness or make excuses) one of the economic formulas of this challenge from a seminar I'm currently teaching on forgiveness, the excuse, and perjury. Here is the formula, bare and very simple in appearance: one only forgives the unforgivable. By only forgiving what is already forgivable, one doesn't forgive anything. Consequently, forgiveness isn't *possible*, *as such*, except where, before the unforgivable, it thus appears *impossible*. As I attempt to show elsewhere more concretely, in a manner that is less formal but more consequential, this enjoins us to think the *possible* (the *possibility* of forgiveness, but also of the gift, of hospitality – and the list is not closed, by definition, it contains all the *unconditionals*) *as the impossible itself*. If the *possible "is" the im-possible here*, if, as I have so often taken the risk of saying about different themes but in a manner that is relatively formalizable, the "condition of possibility" is a "condition of impossibility", how then must the thinking of the possible be rethought, the thinking that comes to us from the depths of our tradition (Aristotle, Leibniz, Kant, Bergson, and so on, and Heidegger also, whose use of the words "*mögen*" and "*Vermögen*", notably in *The Letter on Humanism*,[11] would merit a separate treatment here)?

How to understand the word "possible?" How to read the negation that is affecting the verb "to be" such that the three words of this proposition "the possible '*is*' the im-possible" are no longer associated by a simple word game, playful paradox or dialectical facility? But how must we understand the fact that that these words come to undermine, in a serious and necessary manner, the very propositionality of this proposition of the type *S is P* (*the possible "is" the im-possible*)? Furthermore, is this a *question*, or a *problem*? And what is the complicity between this thinking of the im-possible possible and the instance of the "perhaps" that I was discussing earlier? Since I already seem to have counted on the distinction between "who" and "what" (answer *to whom*? before *whom*? but also *for what*? and *what*?), in order to make it tremble a little, permit me to specify that, in my current work, and especially in my teaching (for example, in the last several years on the subject of the gift, the secret, witnessing, hospitality, forgiveness, the excuse, the oath, and perjury), I'm trying to achieve a position *from* which this distinction between "who" and "what" begins to appear and determine itself, in other words a place "anterior" to this distinction, a place "older" or "younger" than it, a place that both compels determination and also makes possible the terribly reversible translation of "who" into "what". Why call this a *place*, a location, a spacing, an interval, a sort of *khora*?

Rules for the Impossible (Aphoristic IV)

I seem to have taken off like a shot, so to speak. I ask once more for forgiveness as I start over, differently.

To respond, if that's the right word, is what Michel Meyer generously asked, or offered, me to do. I was imprudent enough to promise to do it and thus to risk perjuring myself. After several appreciative readings of all these strong, lucid and generous texts, my delay will only have been that of an anxious, feverish race, more and more slow and more and more fast. Slower and faster at once: try to understand that. A haste then took hold, and, as they say, I was racing toward failure. I was headed for disaster, which I could see coming more and more clearly without being able to do anything about it. Obviously, I didn't want the silence of a simple non-response to be interpreted – wrongly, of course – as haughtiness or ingratitude. But just as obviously, I couldn't, with a limited amount of time and a proportionally reduced number of pages, "within such limits" (Austin), claim to respond to so many texts so different in their approach, their style, the works treated, the problematics elaborated, to so many addresses that were so demanding by the force and the *acribie* of the questions, the richness of their propositions and the depth of the concerns for which they assume the responsibility. A sort of philosophical irresponsibility would have been added to the insufficient sufficiency of any brief or rapid response.

Certainly, I will escape neither one nor the other. At least, perhaps, I will have begun by admitting the failure and the fault – and by asking for forgiveness. If only to add a little – precisely on the subject of forgiving – to the suggestion I made a moment ago. Once the *possibility* of forgiveness, if there is one, consists of a certain *im-possibility*, must one conclude that it is necessary to *do the impossible*? And do it with words, only with words? Must one do the impossible for forgiveness to arrive as such? Perhaps, but this could never be established as a law, a norm, a rule or obligation. There shouldn't be any *il faut* (one must) for forgiveness. Forgiveness "must" remain unmotivated and unpredictable. One never gives or forgives "in accordance with duty" (*pflichtmässig*) or even "from duty" (*eigentlich aus Pflicht*), to use the good Kantian distinction. One forgives, if one forgives, beyond any categorical imperative, beyond debt and obligation. And yet one *should* (*il faudrait*) forgive. What is the actual assumption of the infinite forgiveness, the "hyperbolic" and unconditional forgiveness, the one from which the "commandment" seems to come to us, by heritage, from the Abrahamic tradition, and is taken up, in different forms, by Saint Paul and the Koran? Does it presuppose, as its condition (condition of unconditionality itself, thus), that forgiveness is asked for and the fault admitted, as Jankelevitch forcefully points out?[12] But then it would no longer be unconditional. Conditional once again, it wouldn't be a pure forgiveness, it would become impossible again, otherwise impossible. Or perhaps it can't be unconditional, and thus possible *as unconditional*, unless it forgives the unforgivable (and thus becomes possible *as* impossible). Can't it only be as it must be, unconditional, when it no longer even demands this confession or this repentance, this exchange, this identification, this economic horizon of reconciliation, redemption and salvation? I would be tempted to think so, at once *in* and *against* this powerful tradition. Under these conditions, what does it mean to "inherit" a tradition, when one thinks from its perspective, in its name, certainly, but precisely *against it in its name*, against the very thing it will have felt obligated to save in order to survive while vanishing? Again the possibility of the impossible: the heritage wouldn't be possible except where it becomes im-possible. This is one of the possible definitions of deconstruction – precisely as an inheritance. I once made this proposal: deconstruction would perhaps be "the experience of the impossible".[13]

I must now, without deferring any longer, without devoting any more space and time introducing so many subjects that I won't treat, present and justify, as much as possible, the rule that I thought I should choose in order to limit the seriousness of this long failure. I wouldn't know how, "within such limits", to respond in a detailed manner to each of the texts that have just been read; it would require at least an article per page. But I can't and don't want to group my answers by general themes, which would blur the pronounced originality of each of the texts which was given me to read. Finally, in none of the texts did I find anything to object to or anything that might make me want to plead a defense for my past work (another way of saying that these texts are not only courteous and generous, but in my eyes impeccable in their reading and the discussion that they will open). I resigned myself, finally, to putting myself forward, me, in other words, to advance, by following several rules, a more or less disconnected series of *quasi*-propositions. Concerning my work in progress and the difficulties through which it still remains to come, these *quasi*-propositions would resonate or reason (*résonneraient ou raisonneraient*); they correspond, by slightly displacing the consonance, to the anxieties, worries and questions of those who do me the honor here of being interested in what it is I have written. Which is to say that, one can already see it, these *quasi*-propositions, limited to a few pages of rigor, will remain, at least at first, *aphoristic*. But is there ever an argumentation free of all discontinuity? It's true that there are leaps and there are leaps. One can plead for some hiatuses: certain ones are worth more than others.

Such aphoristic *quasi*-propositions are and will remain *oblique* in their relation to the texts with which I will none the less attempt to make them agree. While doing everything to respond *precisely beside the point*. But this doesn't mean that I'll yield to some *oratio obliqua* or that I'll try to prevaricate. Even where it seems impossible, and precisely there, directness, as I said earlier, remains *de rigeur*. Inflexibly. If I've multiplied the detours and the contortions, including when I humbly ask forgiveness and commiseration for doing it, it's because here I am, I am placed, I have placed myself, in an untenable position and before an impossible task. Forgiveness and pity: *mercy*.[14]

Yes to Hospitality: (Aphoristic V)

The *problems* with the response and the delay have thus just declared themselves. Having read Michel Meyer, do I still have the right to refer to them thus, to call them "problems"? And an instant ago I spoke imprudently of "propositions". To specify, as I did, "*quasi*-propositions", is undoubtedly to demonstrate an attention to precisely the problem of propositionalism that is emphasized by Meyer.[15] But this *quasi*, all by itself, doesn't advance things much at all. Another concept would be necessary. I have never found a concept that can be contained in one word. Should one be surprised? Has there ever been a concept that is truly namable? I mean namable with just one name or just one word? The concept always demands sentences, discourses, work and process: text, in a word. For example, *khora* undoubtedly doesn't designate the same concept in the *Timaeus* as in the *Republic* (516b, passage cited by Sallis). One could say it's only a homonym, almost another word. The consequences of this necessity (or of what I hold in any case to be an unavoidable experience) appear to me to be formidable yet inescapable. I sometimes have the impression of having done nothing, ever, but try to be coherent in this regard. Perhaps I've just wanted to take note, quite simply, of this necessity and testify to it.

But there's nothing fortuitous in the fact that the modality of "*quasi*" (or the logico-rhetorical fiction of "as if") has so often seemed essential to me to turn a word into a sentence, and primarily, especially, as has often been noted and commented on, concerning the word "transcendental". A question of problematic context and strategy, no doubt: one must *here* reaffirm, without respite, the transcendental type of question, and *there*, almost simultaneously, wonder about the history and limits of what is called "transcendental". But above all else, the essential possibility of an "as if" has to be taken into account, an "as if" that affects all language and all experience with a *possible* fictionality, fantasmaticity, spectrality. This word "transcendental" is not an example among others. The category of "quasi-transcendental" has played a deliberately equivocal yet determinant role in a number of my essays. Rodolphe Gasché has proposed a powerful interpretation of it.[16] Of course, the use of "quasi" and of "ultra-transcendental"[17] to which I had to resolve myself is still, and already was, a manner of saving, even as I betrayed it, the legacy of philosophy, namely the demand for the condition of possibility (for the a priori, for what is originary or the foundation, so many different forms of the same radical exigency of every philosophical "question"); to use these terms was also to get involved, without concealing from myself the difficulty, in the task of thinking further about what the "possible" means, like the "impossible", and to do it in terms of the aforementioned "condition of possibility," often shown to be the "condition of impossibility". Thus what is said about the condition of possibility is also valid, by analogy, for the "foundation," the "origin", the "root" of "radicality", and so on.

Even before I began to name them in admitting my fault, the related *problems* of the response and of the delay were treated by at least three of my colleagues: by Michel Meyer (who puts back into play the question of the question, and therefore the question of the answer, of "answerhood" equated with "propositionality" – "answerhood, that is propositionality" – but also of "problematological difference" as "*différance* . . . when we leave propositionalism" – and *différance* is also a sort of originary delay), by Daniel Giovannangeli (who recalls everything that belatedness, or *Nachträglichkeit*, governs, when this "anachrony", the "anachrony of time itself" ... "encloses and exceeds philosophy"),[18] finally by John Sallis (for whom the question or the answer of the return to things themselves, to philosophy *itself*, presupposes, like "the very opening in question", the opening of an interval that delays (and lags behind) (*retarde* [*sur*]) imminence itself: "to intend to begin, to be about to begin, is also to delay, to defer the very beginning that one is about to make" – which, as has you may have suspected for some time now, I have been doing here, without complacency.

Answer and delay, then: an answer, at least according to good sense, is always second and secondary. It lags behind the question or the request, behind the expectation in any case. And yet everything starts with an answer. If I had to resume, using an elliptical paradox, the thought that has not ceased to traverse everything that I say and write,[19] I would talk about an originary answer: the "yes" everywhere where this indispensable acquiescence is implied (in other words, everywhere where one speaks and addresses oneself to the other, if only to deny, to argue, to oppose oneself, and so on), is first of all a response. To say "yes" is to respond. But nothing precedes this answer. Nothing precedes its delay – and therefore its anachrony.

Coming *after* them, after the texts and the authors that have just been read, without judging it possible or necessary to do anything other than to listen to them, and to ask that they be read and reread, I'll just describe the movement I'm embarking on from this perspective. Although I never limit it to the propositional form (in the necessity of which I also believe, of course), I've never felt obliged (not that anyone could or must be able to) to give up the question, any form of question, a certain "primacy of questioning" (Michel Meyer), or what connects the question to the problem, to *problematization*. Is there ever a question free of every problem, that is to say of all elaboration, of all syntax, of all articulable differentiality, on the one hand, but also, on the other hand, of all self-protection? Because problematization is certainly the only *consequential* organization of a question, its grammar and its semantic, but also it is a first apotropaic measure to protect it against the barest of questions, at once the most inflexible and the most unprotected, the question of the other when it calls me into question at the moment it addresses itself to me. I've tried elsewhere to account for this "shield" of the "*problema*". The *problema* also designates "the substitute, the replacement, the prosthesis, the thing or the person that one *puts forward* to protect oneself by hiding, the thing (or person) (ce[lui]) that comes in the place or in the name of the other".[20]

Problematization is already an articulated organization of the response. This is valid everywhere, in particular in the history of philosophical and scientific configurations. By whatever name they go by, and however one interprets them (paradigm, *epistémè*, *themata*, and so on), these historical configurations that form the basis of questions are already possibilities of answers. They pre-organize, they make possible the event, the apparent invention, the surging forth and the elaboration of questions, their problematization, the reappropriation that momentarily renders them determinable and treatable.

There is – there, in the inevitability of the question – not just an essence of philosophy but an unconditional right and obligation, the joint foundation of philosophy as science and as law (*droit*). Insofar as this unconditionality is being recalled precisely where it goes without saying, I must also specify this: although I've never ceased to deploy everything I've written as a *question of the question*,[21] this very *necessity* is not reduced to the question. The double necessity, the double law of the ineluctable and the imperative injunction (*il faut*), exceeds the question at the very moment that it reaffirms its necessity. By so often confirming that everything begins not with the question but with the answer, with a "yes, yes"[22] which is originarily an answer to the other, it is a matter not of putting this unconditionality into question once again, so to speak, but of imagining both its possibility and its impossibility, one *as* the other.

Nearly thirty-five years ago, I was already inquiring about (would I say that at the time I was *questioning* myself on this subject?) "unanswerable questions".[23]

> By right of birth, and for one time at least, these are problems put to philosophy as problems philosophy cannot resolve.
> It may even be that these questions are not *philosophical*, are not *philosophy's* questions. Nevertheless, these should be the only questions today capable of founding the community, within the world, of those who are still called philosophers; and called such in remembrance, at very least, that these questions must be examined unrelentingly ... A community of the question, therefore, within that fragile moment when the question is not yet determined enough for the hypocrisy of an answer to have already *initiated* itself beneath the mask of the question, and not yet determined enough for its voice to have been already and fraudulently articulated within the very syntax of the question ... A community of the question about the possibility of the question. This is very little – almost nothing – but within it, today, is sheltered and encapsulated an unbreachable dignity and duty of *decision*. An unbreachable responsibility.
> Why unbreachable? Because the *impossible has already* occurred ... there is a history of the question ...The question has already begun ... A founded dwelling, a realized tradition of the question remaining a question ... correspondence of the question with itself ...[24]

Please forgive me this long quote from an old text. Will I say, once more, that I am excusing myself for it? Beyond the weakness of which I could be accused, I wanted first to acknowledge a trajectory that at least cuts across – as it has for such a long time – many of the "problematological" motives elaborated by Michel Meyer, especially when he writes precisely that "Problematicity is historicity". But, surprised myself (can I admit this without seeming too naive or stupidly reassured in the face of what might be nothing but immobility and monotony?) by the insistence and consistency of this statement, and by the continuity of its displacement, I especially wanted to localize the new motives which, without rupture, because they haven't ceased to occupy me in my seminars for the last few years, haven't yet been touched upon, even here, in the collected texts. Indeed, I had announced my hope – rather than *to respond* to all the essays in this volume – *to correspond* with them by situating certain difficulties of my work in progress. The words emphasized in the quotation I've just made are first of all indications in this respect, and paths for me; they signal toward the themes and problems that besiege me today: another way of thinking the limit of the philosophical in the face of questions like *hospitality* (*invitation/visitation*, and a whole chain of associated subjects: the *promise, testimony*, the *gift, forgiveness*, and so on), but also the test of an im-possible that wouldn't be negative. Such a test implies another thinking of the event, of the "taking place": only the im-possible takes place, and the deployment of a potentiality or a possibility that is already there will never make an event or an invention. What is valid for the event is also valid for the decision, thus for responsibility: a decision that I *am able* to make, a decision that is *in my power* and which shows the passage to the act or the deployment of what is *already possible* for me, the actualization of my possible, a decision that only depends on me: would this still be a decision? From this there emerges the paradox without paradox to which I'm trying to give myself over: the responsible decision must be this im-possible possibility of a "passive" decision, a decision of the other in me who will not exempt me from any freedom or from any responsibility.

Necessity of the Impossible (Aphoristic VI)

I've devoted numerous analyses of the aporetic type to "the singular modality of this 'impossible'". Concerning the *gift*, notably, in *Given Time*:

> ... one can think, desire, and say only the impossible, according to the measureless measues [*mesure* sans *mesure*] of the impossible. If one wants to recapture the proper element of thinking, naming, desiring, it is perhaps according to the measureless measure of this limit that it is possible, possible as relation *without* relation to the impossible. One can desire, name, think in the proper sense of these words, if there is one, *only* to the *immeasuring* extent [*dans la mesure* démesurante] that one desires, names, thinks *still* or *already*, that one still lets announce itself what nevertheless cannot *present itself* as experience, to knowing: in short, here *a gift that cannot make itself (a) present* [un don qui ne peut se faire présent].[25]

The figure of "given time" was named long before this, and emphasized.[26] It followed the elaboration of the "possibility of the impossible," which was then set forth as another name for time:

> But it has already been remarked that this impossibility, when barely formulated, contradicts itself, is experienced as the possibility of the impossible ... Time is a name for this impossible possibility.[27]

Later, the concept of the invention obeyed the same "logic":

> Invention is always possible, it is the invention of the possible ... Thus it is that invention would be in conformity with its concept, with the dominant feature of the word and concept "invention", only insofar as, paradoxically, invention invents nothing, when in invention the other does not come, and when nothing comes to the other or from the other. For the other is not the possible. So it would be necessary to say that the only possible invention would be the invention of the impossible. But an invention of the impossible is impossible, the other would say. Indeed. But it is the only possible invention: an invention has to declare itself to be the invention of that which did not appear to be possible; otherwise, it only makes explicit a program of possibilities within the economy of the same.[28]

In the interval, *The Post Card*[29] entails the same necessity in the direction of destination (*à destination de la destination*), of the very concept of destination. Once a letter *can not arrive* at its destination, it is impossible for it to arrive *fully*, or *simply*, at a single destination. The im-possibility, the possible as im-possible, is always linked to an irreducible divisibility that affects the very essence of the possible. Whence the insistance on the divisibility of the letter and its destination:

> The divisibility of the letter – this is why we have insisted on this key or theoretical safety lock of the Seminar – is what chances and sets off course, without guarantee of reture, the remaining [*restance*] of anything whatsoever: a letter does not always arrive at its destination, and from the moment that this possibility belongs to its structure one can say that it never truly arrives, that when it does arrive its capacity not to arrive torments it with an internal drifting.[30]

Why this allusion to *torment*? It names a suffering and a passion, an affect both sad and joyous, the instability of an anxiety proper to all possibilization, which allows itself to be haunted by the spectre of its impossibility, by mourning for itself: a self-mourning carried within itself, but which also gives it its life or its survival, its very possibility. Because this *im*-possibility opens its possibility, it leaves a trace, both a chance and a threat, *within* that which it makes possible. The torment would sign this scar, the trace of this trace. But this is also said, in *The Post Card*, about the "impossible decision", that appears to be impossible insofar as it depends entirely on the other.[31] (This subject was largely explained in *Politics of Friendship*.) It can also be found in terms of Freud and the concept of *Bemächtigung*, of the limit or the paradoxes of the possible as power.[32]

There is nothing fortuitous in the fact that this discourse on the conditions of possibility – in the very place where its pretention is obsessed with the impossibility of overcoming its own performativity – can be extended to all the places where some performative force happens or causes to happen (advient ou fait advenir) (the event, the invention, the gift, forgiveness, hospitality, friendship, the promise, the experience of death – possibility of the impossible, impossibility of the possibile, experience in general, etc. *Et cetera*, because the contagion is without limit; it eventually leads to all concepts and undoubtedly the concept of the concept, etc.).

Promising to respond straightforwardly (*dans la droiture*), thus *just beside* the point: the possible-impossible. Recalling that on the untenable line of this possible-impossible everything I've ever been able to write in the name of *destinerrance* has been written, and this was always at the crossing of many of the routes sketched out and reinterpreted by the texts assembled here. The risk of misunderstanding, the errancy of an answer beside the point: all this must always remain possible in this exercise of straightforwardness. There wouldn't be any straightforwardness, any ethic of the discussion otherwise. But what I'm proposing here is not intended, any more than were my earlier allusions to responsibility, to hospitality, to the gift, to forgiveness, to testifying, and so on, to outline some "ethical turn",[33] as some have said. I'm simply trying to pursue with some consequence the thinking that for many years has been engaged in the same aporias. The question of ethics, of law and of politics didn't spring forth unexpectedly, like at a bend in the road. Furthermore, the manner in which this question is usually discussed isn't reassuring in terms of a "moral" – and perhaps because it asks too much of it.

The possibility of this evil (the misunderstanding, the miscomprehension, the mistake) is, in its own way, a chance. It gives time. There must be the "there must be" of the error ("*Il faut donc le 'il faut' du défaut*"), and adequation must remain *impossible*. But there's nothing negative, ontologically, in this "there must be fault" (*ce "il faut du défaut"*). It must be obligatory, if one prefers, that *in*adequacy remains *always possible* so for interpretation in general, and the answer, in turn, to be *possible*. Here is an example of this law that connects the possible to the impossible. Because an interpretation without fault, a totally adequate self-comprehension, wouldn't just mark the end of a history exhausted by its very transparence. By prohibiting the future, it would make everything *impossible*, both the event and the coming of the other, the coming to the other (*la venue à l'autre*) – and thus the response, the very "yes" of the response, the "yes" *as* response. The answer can only be adjusted in an exceptional fashion, and even then there is no prior, objective criterion to assure oneself of it, to assure oneself that the exception is really taking place *as* an exception.

Perhaps the haunting of the exception indicates a passage, if not the way out. I do mean to say haunting, because the spectral structure here is the law, both of the possible and the impossible, of their strange intertwining. The exception is always *de rigeur*. This applies, perhaps, to the stubborness of "perhaps," in its elusive modality which is irreducible to any other, fragile and yet indestructible. "Quasi" or "as if," "perhaps," "spectrality" of the *phantasma* (which also means the "ghost"), these are the components of another thinking of the virtual, of a virtuality that no linger organizes itself according to the traditional notion of the possible (*dynamis, potentia, possibilitas*). When the impossible *makes itself* possible, the event takes place (possibility *of* the impossible). This is, without question, is the paradoxal form of the event: if an event is only possible, in the classic sense of the word, if it inscribes itself in the conditions of possibility, if it does no more than make explicit, unveil, reveal, accomplish what was already possible, then it's no longer an event. For an event to take place, for it to be possible, it must be, as event, as invention, the coming of the impossible. There is a simple notion, a notion that is nothing less than obvious. It's what has incessantly guided me between the possible and the impossible. It has also inspired me so often to talk about the *condition of impossibility*. What's at stake, then, is nothing less than the powerful concept of the *possible* that traverses Western thought from Aristotle to Kant to Husserl (then differently in Heidegger), with all of its virtual or potential significations: the being-in-power (*l'être-en-puissance*), precisely, the *dynamis*, virtuality (in its classic and modern forms, pre-technical and technical), but also power, capacity, anything that entitles or empowers, and so on. The choice of this set of themes possesses a strategic value, certainly, but it also carries a movement to push even further, beyond all calculable strategy. It carries what is called deconstruction toward a terrifying question, tormenting it from the inside, at once the most powerful and the most precarious axiom (impotent in its very potence) of the dominant thought of the possible in philosophy (thus subjugated in the power of its very dominance).

But how is it possible, one will ask, that that which makes possible makes impossible the very thing that it makes possible, thus, and introduces – as its chance – a non-negative chanciness, a principle of ruin into the very thing it promises and promotes? The *im-* of the im-possible is without a doubt radical, implacable, undeniable. But it isn't simply negative or dialectical: it *introduces* the possible, and acts *today as its gatekeeper*; it makes it come and makes it turn either according to an anachronic temporality or according to an incrcedible filiation – which is, furthermore, also the origin of faith. Because it exceeds knowledge and conditions the address to the other, inscribes all theorems into the space and time of a testimony ("I'm talking to you, believe me"). In other words – and this is the introduction to an aporia without example, an aporia of logic rather than a logical aporia – here is an impasse of the undecidable by which a decision can't not pass. All responsibility must pass by this aporia which, far from paralyzing it, puts in motion a new notion of the possible. It insures its rhythm and its respiration: diastolic, systolic, syncopated, the heartbeat of the *im*-possible possible, of the impossible as the condition of the possible. From the very heart of the im-possible, one can hear the drive and the pulse of a "deconstruction".

The condition of possibility thus gives the possible a chance, but by depriving it of its purity. The law of this spectral contamination, the impure law of this impurity, this is what must be constantly re-elaborated. For example: the possibility of failure isn't simply inscribed, like a prior risk, into the condition of possibility of success of a performative (a promise must *be able not to* be kept, it must threaten not to be kept or to become a threat in order to be freely given, and even to succeed;[34] from this comes the originary inscription of culpability, of the confession, of the excuse and of forgiveness in the promise). The possibility of failure must continue to mark the event, even when it succeeds, like the trace of an impossibility, at times its memory and always its haunting. This im-possibility is thus not the simple contrary of the possible. It seems opposed to it but it also gives itself over to possibility: this impossibility traverses possibility and leaves in it the trace of its withdrawal. An event wouldn't be worthy of its name, it wouldn't make anything happen, if it did nothing but deploy, make explicit, actualize what was already possible, that is to say, in sum, if all it did was to implement a program or apply a general rule to a specific case. For there to be an event, it has to be possible, of course, but there must also be an exceptional, absolutely singular interruption in the regime of possibility; the event must not be *simply* possible; it must not reduce itself to the explication, the unfolding, the acting out of a possible. The event, if there is one, isn't the actualization of a possible, a simple acting out, a realization, an effectuation, the teleological accomplishment of a power, the process of a dynamic that depends on "conditions of possibility". The event has nothing to do with history, if one understands history as a teleological process. It must interrupt in a certain manner this kind of history. It's according to these premises that I was able to speak, particularly in *Specters of Marx*, of messianicity without messianism. *It is imperative* (*il faut*) then that the event declare itself impossible or that its possibility be threatened.

But then why this "it is imperative", one might ask. What is the status of this necessity, of this apparently contradictory yet doubly obligatory law? What is this "double bind" on the basis of which the possible *should* (*il faudrait*) once more be rethought as *im*-possible?

It may be a necessity that escapes the habitual regime of necessity (*ananké, Notwendigkeit*), necessity understood as natural law or law of liberty. For one can't imagine the possibility of the impossible otherwise without rethinking necessity. The analyses that concern the event and the performative – and the scope of which we've just been reminded – I've also attempted such analyses, in an analogous manner, over the course of the last fifteen years, in particular concerning destination, testimony, invention, the gift, forgiveness, that which connects hospitality to the im-possible promise, to the pervertibility of the performative in general, and so on – and in particular, concerning death, the aporicity of the aporia in general. This pervertibility is less transcendental in that it doesn't affect the classical reflection on the transcendental, or on the transcendental "condition of possibility" in all its forms: medieval ontotheology, criticism or phenomenology.[35] It doesn't delegitimize transcendental questioning, it de-limits and questions its original historicity. For nothing can discredit the right to the transcendental or ontological question. It is the only force that resists empiricism and relativism. Despite appearances, toward which impatient philosophers seem to throw themselves, nothing is less empiricist or relativist than a certain attention to the multiplicity of contexts and discursive strategies that these govern, a certain insistence on the fact that a context is always open and can't be saturated, a taking account of the "perhaps" and the "quasi" in a thinking of the event, and so on.

Transaction and Event (Aphoristic VII)

There is in this insistant displacement of the strategy and the non-strategy (in other words, of the vulnerable exposure to that which happens), something like a *transaction*. One negotiates, one comes to terms *with* and *on* the limit of philosophy as such. This limit takes the double form of a *différantial* (*différantielle*) logic of analogy: on one hand the "quasi", the "as if", of a *différance* that maintains the delay, the relay, the return, and the term given in the economy of the same; and the rupture, on the other hand, the event of the im-possible, *différance* as *diaphora*, the aphorismic experience of absolute heterogeniety. On one hand the concatenation of syllogistic sequences, on the other, but "at the same time," the seriality of aphoristic sequences.

Karel Thein is thus correct to guide his rich analysis of the analogy, in "Plato's Pharmacy", to the point where the question pertains, and precisely with the agency (*instance*) of the decision, to what he calls "the conditions and the limits of the analogy as such". The interpretation I'm attempting of the *khora* comes to perturb the regime of the analogy. As John Sallis so correctly emphasizes (in our ongoing dialogue about Plato's text which, for years, has meant so much, a text which we both feel possesses an implosive power which it keeps in reserve), this is also valid for that which, in the definition of the Good and of the *epekeina tes ousias* as beyond being, would remain in a sort of ana-onto-logy. It's about another excess. The "other time" that Sallis emphasizes is also what governs all the tests (*épreuves*) I was talking about earlier (the im-possible, the passive decision, the "perhaps," the event as absolute interruption of the possible, etc.). All of Sallis's questions certainly seem legitimate to me, as do the answers he gives them ("Can there be, then, a metaphorizing of the *khora*? If not, then how is one to read the passage of the *khora* of the sun ...? How is the *khora* itself – if there be a *khora* itself – to be beheld? What is the difference marked by the as [in the hypothesis where *khora* is perceived 'as in a dream']?") But these legitimate answers are subject to the law of the philosophical, which is dominated by the necessity of the ana-onto-logy (which are those of ontology but also of phenomenology, that is to say of the appearence as such of the *as such* (*comme tel du* comme tel), of the *as*).[36] But the rupture that interests me in the reading of the *khora*, as I risked it, is that *khora* becomes the name of that which never allows itself to be metaphorized, in spite of the fact that *khora* is both can and cannot give rise to so many analogical figures. The *khora* of the sun, in the *Republic*, is not, it seems to me, able to be a metaphorical value for *khora* in the *Timaeus*. Nor, for that matter, the inverse. Although the word clearly designates, in both cases, an "emplacement" or a "locality", there is no analogy, no commensurability possible, it seems to me, between these two places. The word "place" itself has such a different semantic value in the two cases that their relation (I believe this and suggested it earlier), seems to be one of homonymy rather than figurality or synonymy. It's on the basis of this conviction that, rightly or wrongly, I treated *khora*, in the *Timaeus*, like a *quasi* proper name. If *Khora* escapes all metaphor, it's not in order to remain inaccessible in its own properness (sa propre propriété), in its ipseity, in the itself of what it is. Rather, earlier (*plutôt, plus tôt*), because that which is there is not the *khora* itself. There is no *khora* itself (as John Sallis correctly suspects when he writes "if there be a khora itself"). I'll concede that this seems very disconcerting. This unicity without properness puts into crisis – here and not necessarily elsewhere – any distinction between figure and non-figure, and therefore this distinction between "literal reading" and "figurative reading",[37] which Michel Meyer is no doubt correct, in other cases, to dissociate as two "steps". There is, here, in the singular case of *khora* (but also in the case of its analogues, which remain nonetheless absolutely singular and different), a name without a referent, without a referent that is a thing or a being (*étant*) or even a phenomenon appearing *as such*. This possibility thus disorganizes the whole regime of the philosophical type of question (ontological or transcendental) without giving in to a pre-philosophical empiricism. It only shows itself as a figure of the impossible which is no longer a figure and which I've tried to show never appears as such.[38] It throws the "as such" off track and deprives it of its status as phenomeno-ontological criterion. I'm trying to explain myself on the necessity of this singular nomination, as well as on its contingency, and on what we inherit here, that is, a name of natural language in its ordinary usage (*khora*), a name both replaceable and irreplaceable. To be replaceable in its very irreplaceability, this is what happens to every singularity, to every proper noun, even and especially when what it names "properly" has no relation of properness that is indivisible to itself, to some *self*[39] which would be properly that which it is *as such*, to some intact ipseity. Prosthesis of the proper noun that comes to signify, to call (without any ontic referent, without anything that appears as such, without object or corresponding being, without a meaning in the world or out of the world) some "thing" that isn't a thing and has no analogical correspondence to anything at all. This nomination is an event (at once impossible and decisive, which we may or may not be able to decide to inherit). But isn't every inagural naming an event? Isn't the giving of a name the performative *par excellence*?

Knowing How to Think *(savoir-penser)*: Inheriting "the critical mission of philosophy" (Aphoristic VII)

Without at all being a "program", what does *différance* "say" or "do"? (It "is" neither a word nor a concept, I once said[40] in obvious denegation, but one whose traces remain, in some sense – to the point of making the denegation of the denegation as legitimate as it is inoperative, as if there were many of us who suspected that this untenable denegation must have wanted to affirm, through its very inconsistency, "something" which would still deserve to be taken seriously.) That which presented itself as "*différance*" had this singular quality: simultaneously welcoming, but without the ease of the dialectic, the same and the other, the economy of the analogy – the same only differed, relayed, put off – *and* the rupture of all analogy, absolute heterology. But one could also, in this context, re-treat this question of *différance* as a question of heritage. The heritage would consist here of remaining faithful to that which is received (and *khora* is also that which receives, the enigma of what "receptacle", *endekhomenon*, might mean and do, in the place where *khora* says nothing and does nothing), while rejecting any figure of that which is received. One must always reject out of faithfulness – and in the name of a heritage that is fatally contradictory in its injunctions. For example, concerning the gift, forgiveness, hospitality, and so on, in the name of the heritage of Abraham, which demands of me a certain hyperbolic unconditionality, I must be willing to break with all economic and conditional reappropriations that incessantly compromise this heritage. But this break itself will still have to conduct transactions and define its necessary conditions in history, law, politics and economics (and economics means economics in the strict sense but also the economy among the different fields) to make this heritage of the hyperbole as effective as possible. From this paradoxical yet easily formalizable necessity, from this break *(still economic)* with economy, from this heterogeneity that interrupts analogy (but *still* lends itself to it in order to make itself understood), I would be tempted to interpret all of the gestures which – precisely here – elaborate in such a clear manner, and against so many prejudices, the commitment of deconstruction, at least as I attempt to practice and interpret it, to science, technique, reason and the Enlightenment. I'm thinking in particular of the demonstrations of Christopher Johnson, Christopher Norris and Arkady Plotnitsky.

We have long been able to follow Norris's work, which is so original, so perseverent and so incisive, against so many misunderstandings and against a host of prejudices as tenacious as they are crudely polemical (deconstruction as "relativist", "skeptical", "nihilist", "irrationalist", "the enemy of the Enlightenment", "a prisoner of spoken language and rhetoric", "unaware of the difference between logic and rhetoric, philosophy and literature", and so on). It's no accident that Norris so often calls for a re-examination of the status of the *analogy* in my work, as he does here again, and the reelaboration of the problem concept/metaphor. I find particularly judicious his strategy, often privileged in all his texts, and here again (a certain passage through "White Mythology" – in relation to Nietzsche, but also to Canguilhem and to Bachelard – and "The Supplement of the Copula"), and particularly effective the re-situation of the demonstrative means (*leviers*) he proposes with respect to Anglo-American developments which he has for a long time helped me to read and to understand (Davidson, for instance). I am not shocked, even if it makes me smile, to see myself defined by Norris, in a deliberately provocative and ironic manner, as a "transcendental realist". Earlier I said why I didn't believe it was necessary to reject the transcendental motive (*motif*). As for the deconstruction of logocentrism, of linguisticism, of economism (of the self and of the at-home [*chez-soi*], oikos, of the same) and so on, as for the affirmation of the impossible, these are always advanced *in the name of the real*, of the irreducible reality of the real – not of the real as attribute of the objective, present, perceptible or intelligible *thing* (*res*), but of the real as the coming or the event of the other, where it resists all reappropriation, even ana-onto-phenomenonological appropriation. The real is this non-negative im-possible, this im-possible coming or invention of the event whose thought is not an onto-phenomenology. It is a thought of the event (singularity of the other, in its unanticipatible coming, *hic et nunc*) that resists its own reappropriation by an ontology or a phenomenology of presence as such. I'm attempting to dissociate the concept of event and the value of presence. It's not easy, but I'm trying to demonstrate this necessity, like that of thinking the event without being (it) (*sans l'être*). Nothing is more "realist," in this sense, than a deconstruction. It is that (whoever) arrives ([*ce*] *qui arrive*). And there is no fatality before the *fait accompli*: neither empiricism nor relativism. Is it to be empiricist or relativist to take into account seriously that which arrives, and the differences of every order, beginning with the difference of context?

Without wanting to reduce all of his richness and the many paths of his demonstrations, I also find it quite remarkable that, when *he too* follows the thread of the analogy, Christopher Johnson first sets apart the word "metaphor". ("The metaphor of writing, as it is articulated with the genetic and the biological in Derrida's texts, is not simply metaphor".) After having proposed "a more discriminating vocabulary" – here the word "isomorphism" – he reorients in a manner that I find very lucid and very sound the very premise of this choice toward another logic or toward another structure, that of the "metaphorical catastrophe," which changes the whole scene and forces a reconsideration of the structure of a semantic inversion or of a conceptual classification. For example: "not only is the term a germ, but the germ is, in the most general sense, a term" (An analysis it would perhaps be fruitful to cross with Karel Thein's discussion of "strong" and "weak" "germs" and of the *sperma athanaton*). It must be remarked that this remarkable analysis finds its privileged horizon in the so-called life sciences, biology and cybernetics (but without yielding to vitalism, as Johnson correctly stresses). But is this just Johnson's choice (which didn't prevent him from opening a rich and diversified field of questioning)? Or, considering what he says at the end of his discussion about the "open" system and its limit, about the necessity of including his own discourse as an example of the system described ("and more than an example", he adds, and I would have liked to ask him to help me imagine this "more than an example"), can one, then, extend what he demonstrates to other sciences, to sciences that would no longer be sciences of the living (*sciences du vivant*)? For instance in the direction indicated by the article and so many other decisive works of Arkady Plotnitsky, concerning the relations between deconstruction and the physical or mathematical sciences? (In the course of this impressive reflection on the folds, positions, points and counterpoints of a certain Hegelian "heritage" of deconstruction, one remarks Plotnitsky's insistence on what he has long held[41] to be a "conceptual" proximity between quantum mechanics, in particular as it is interpreted by Niels Bohr, and a certain theoretical strategy, a certain relation to the calculated risk in deconstructive practice. The theme of the "strategy" receives here an attention which I believe to be justified and determinant.)

I also wonder, without at all making an objection, how to determine the "outside" of science that Johnson talks about, and what name to give to that which he calls a "position *outside* of science". When he recognizes, and rightfully attributes to me, the intention of taking a step beyond a certain boundary of scientific discourse "by taking the notion of the open system to its logical limit, including his own discourse as an example, and more than an example, of the system he describes", is this still a philosophical gesture, as Johnson seems to think, "the critical mission of philosophy"? Or is it a gesture that also passes the closure of philosophy, philosophical discourse finding itself in this respect on the same side as scientific discourse? I admit that I have no simple, stable answer to this question. And this is also due to the somewhat invaginated structure of this limit, of this form of boundary that includes without integrating, if I may say so, the outside in the inside. Plotnitsky nicely sets out the paradoxes of the limit in this respect. Sometimes, it's in the name of classical philosophical demands (transcendental, phenomenological, ontological) that I find it necessary to determine certain limits of scientific discourse. More often, it's in the name of something that I call, for the sake of convenience, the "thought" (*pensée*) (distinct at once from knowledge, from philosophy and from faith), that I look for this position of exteriority. But this word "thought" doesn't completely satisfy me, for several reasons. First, it recalls a Heideggerian gesture (*das Denken*, which is neither philosophy nor science nor faith) which certainly interests me very much and whose necessity I clearly see but to which I still can't completely subscribe, especially when he upholds declarations like "science doesn't think." Secondly, the traditional semantic of the word "*pensée*", its figure or its etymological values (*la pesée* [weighing], *l'examen* [the examination], and so on) doesn't satisfy me unreservedly either. Finally, I attempted long ago to justify, in a manner less simple than certain impatient readers were led to believe, the statement according to which "In a certain manner, 'the thought' doesn't mean anything ... This thought has no weight. It is, in the play of the system, the very thing which never has weight".[42] Yes, "in a certain sense", at least.

As one suspects, this isn't only about label, title, or terminology. When Johnson uses three words ("thought", "philosophy", "science")[43] to situate the most obscure border difficulty, he clearly designates the burdensome effort I insist on imposing on myself in order to mark and *cross* these borders: cross them in the sense that *to cross* is to exceed and pass to the other side, to exceed the limit by confirming it, by taking it into account, but also in the sense that *to pass* is to not let oneself be detained at a border, not to take a border for a border, for an impassable opposition between two heterogeneous domains. This double "logic" of the limit is what I've been trying to formalize by means of the "responses" I've been sketching out here, from one aphoristic sequence to another. I believe, therefore, that the orders of thought and philosophy, even if they don't allow themselves to be reduced to the order of scientific knowledge, nonetheless aren't simply exterior to it, both because they receive what is essential from it and because they are able, from the other side of the limit, to have effects on the inside of the scientific field (I have also tried elsewhere to articulate the order of "faith" here as well).[44] Scientific progress or invention answers the philosophical "type" of questions as well. This is why these *différantial* limits never signify oppositional limits or exclusions. This I will never say "science doesn't think". How not to be extremely grateful to Johnson, Norris and Plotnitsky, for having not just understood, argued, elaborated, but for having deployed this gesture in an original way every time? As all the authors of this group have done, they have carried and explored its necessity well beyond the point to which I ever could have pretended to myself.

Notes

[1] "*Le dernier mot*," then "*Le tout dernier mot*," on Kafka in *L'amitié* (Paris: Gallimard, 1971) and "*Le dernier mot*" in *Après coup* (1935–36), (Paris: Minuit, 1983): "the echo of the word *il y a*". "'There, without a doubt, is the last word' I thought as I listened to them" (66).

[2] Notably in *Politics of Friendship*, trans. George Collins (London: Verso, 1997, Chs 2 and 3), in the wake of this "dangerous perhaps" of which Nietzsche said that it was the thought of philosophers of the future (*l'a-venir*). For example (and I emphasize thus certain words while taking, from the beginning, a precaution: the quotes that I may make from certain of my texts are only intended here to open the space of a discussion. I only hope to prolong this discussion beyond certain limits within which it must remain here, for lack of space, constrained and restrained. These quotes, which I force myself to make against my nature and at the deliberately-run risk of being accused of overconfidence, are in my mind neither arguments of authority nor abusive exhibitions, nor reminders for the authors of the articles published here. They have no need for that. I would just like, in a brief and economical fashion, to address myself, by means of these quotes and references, to the reader who, concerned with pursuing the exchange begun here, would like to consult the texts in concerned): "Now the thought of the 'perhaps' perhaps engages the only possible thought of the event – of friendship to come and friendship for the future. For to love friendship, it is not enough to know how to bear the other in mourning; one must love the future. And there is no more just category for the future than that of the 'perhaps.'" Such a thought conjoins friendship, the future, and the *perhaps* to open on to the coming of what comes – that is to say, necessarily in the regime of a possible whose possibilization must

prevail over the impossible. For a possible that would only be possible (non-impossible), a possible surely and certainly possible, accessible in advance, would be a poor possible, a futureless possible, a possible already *set aside*, so to speak, life-insured. This would be a programme or a causality, a development, a process without an event. The possibilization of the impossible possible must remain at one and the same time as undecidable – and therefore as decisive – as the future itself" (29). "Without the opening of an absolutely undetermined possible, without the radical abeyance and suspense marking a *perhaps*, there would never be either event or decision. Certainly. But nothing takes place and nothing is ever decided without suspending the *perhaps* while keeping its living possibility in living memory. If no decision (ethical, juridical, political) is possible without interrupting determination by engaging oneself in the perhaps, on the other hand, the same decision must interrupt the very thing that is its condition of possibility: the *perhaps* itself" (67).

The quotation marks around the word "living" signal the necessary connection between this risky aporetic of the *possible-im-possible* and a thinking of spectrality (*neither* alive *nor* dead, but alive *and* dead).

3   English in the original.
4   English in the original.
5   English in the original.
6   English in the original.
7   Cf. for example, *How to Do Things with Words*. On this impurity, as it can be otherwise understood, I too have attempted to draw some consequences (in *Limited Inc* and elsewhere). I could, if the time and the space for the exercise were given to me, connect this idea to almost all of my thinking.
8   J.L. Austin, "A Plea for Excuses", in *Philosophical Papers* (Oxford: Oxford University Press, 1961) 175.
9   English in the original.
10   English in the original.
11   One would have to reconstitute and problematize here the context in which propositions such as this appear: "To embrace a 'thing' or a 'person' in its essence means to love it, to favor it. Thought in a more original way such favoring [*Mögen*] means to bestow essence as a gift. Such favoring is the proper essence of enabling, which not only can achieve this or that but also can let something essentially unfold in its provenance, that is, let it be. It is on the 'strength' of such enabling by favoring that something is properly able to be. This enabling is what is properly 'possible' [*das Mögliche*], that whose essence resides in favoring. From this favoring Being enables thinking. The former makes the latter possible. Being is the enabling-favoring, the 'may-be' [*das 'Mog-liche'*]. As the element, Being is the 'quiet power' of the favoring-enabling, that is, of the possible. Of course, our words *möglich* [possible] and *Möglichkeit* [possibility] under the dominance of 'logic' and 'metaphysics', are thought solely in contrast to 'actuality'; that is, they are thought on the basis of a definite – the metaphysical – interpretation of Being as *actus* and *potentia*, a distinction identified with the one between *extentia* and *essentia*", Martin Heidegger, "Letter on Humanism", in *Basic Writings*, trans. David Farrell Krell (New York: Harper and Row, 1977) 196. On these problems, see Richard Kearney's remarkable work *La poétique du possible* (Vrin, 1984). As for a certain thinking of the "more impossible" or of the "more than impossible" as possible ("*Das überunmöglischste ist möglich*", Angelus Silesius), I'll allow myself to refer to *Sauf le nom* (Galilée, 1993, p. 32sq.). All the aporias of the possible-impossible or of the more-than-impossible thus "inhabit," while also making uninhabitable "within" ("*logées*" *mais aussi délogeantes "dedans"*) what one calmly refers to as desire, love, the movement toward the Good, and so on.
12   For instance in *Le Pardon*, (Aubier Montaigne, 1967) 204 and "Nous a-t-on demandé pardon?", in *L'imprescriptible* (1948-1971) (Paris: Seuil, 1986) 47.

[13] "the most rigorous deconstruction has never characterized itself as either foreign to literature or, especially, as something that is *possible* ... it loses nothing by admitting its own impossibility, and those who might be given to premature celebration won't lose anything by waiting. The danger for the deconstructive task would be, rather, *possibility*, and to become a collection of regulated procedures, methodological practices, and accessible formulas. If the force and the desire of deconstruction have a significance, it's a certain experience of the impossible ... the experience of the other as the invention of the impossible, or in other words, the only possible invention", "Psyche: Inventions of the Other", trans. Catherine Porter, in Lindsay Waters and Wlad Godzich, eds, *Reading de Man Reading* (Minneapolis: University of Minnesota Press, 1989) 36.

[14] English in the original.

[15] "We should be more *radical* than deconstruction, and completely leave the realm of propositionalism. Derrida's thought *invites* us to do so." I've emphasized two words here.

I emphasize on one hand the word "invite" for reasons that will become clear later, I hope. Must one say that unconditional hospitality, hospitality at once pure and im-possible, answers to a *logic of the invitation* (when the ipseity of the at-home [*chez-soi*] welcomes the other into its own horizon, when it poses its conditions, claiming thus to know whom it wants to receive, to expect and to invite, and *how, up to what point, whom* it is *possible* for it to invite, etc.) or to a *logic of the visitation* (the host then says *yes* to the coming or to the *unexpected and unpredictable* event of whoever comes, at any moment, early or late, in absolute anachrony, without being invited, without being announced, without any horizon of expectation – like a messiah who is so difficult to identify and so difficult to anticipate that the very name of messiah, the figure of the messiah, and especially of messianism, would reveal again a haste in ranking the invitation above the visitation). How to conform to the meaning of *what* we call an event, namely the unanticipatible coming of *that* which comes (*ce qui vient*) and of *whoever* comes (*qui vient*), the meaning of the event being nothing other than the meaning of the other, the meaning of absolute alterity? The *invitation* maintains control and receives within the limits of the possible; thus it isn't pure hospitality; rations hospitality, it still belongs to the order of the judicial and the political; the *visitation*, calls forth a pure and unconditional hospitality that welcomes what happens as im-possible. The only possible hospitality, as pure hospitality, should thus do the impossible. How would this im-possible be possible? How would it become so? What is the best transaction – economic or aneconomic – between the logic of the invitation and the logic of the visitation? Between their analogy and their heterology? What, then, is experience, if it is this becoming-possible of the impossible as such as? I'm not sure whether I've practiced or preferred the invitation, rather than the wait without expectation of the visitation, but I won't swear to anything.

On the other hand, I also emphasize the word *radical*, namely the powerful metaphysical subject of radicality of which the word recalls the necessity. One thinks of figures of the root, of depth, of the origin that is said to be radical, and so on, from Aristotle (for whom causes are "roots") to Husserl – and of all the "foundationalisms," as they say in the world of Anglo-Saxon thought, in the course of debates to which I've never been able, I admit it, to adapt my premises. Because, feeling myself to be both foundationalist and anti-foundationalist, from one problematic context to another, from one interrogative strategy to another, I don't know how to use the "word" *in general*: in general I am and remain "*quasi-foundationalist*". This motive of radicality, as figure and as an irrecusable injunction, isn't it precisely what is submitted to the turbulence of a deconstruction? Deconstruction has never laid claim to radicalism and in any case never consisted in raising the stakes of radicality. The fact remains that an excess in this direction can certainly not do any harm (radicalism is in fact to be recommended to all philosophers, it is undoubtedly philosophy itself) but it might not alter the terrain, alter the terrain already subjected the seismic turbulence I've just mentioned. That's why, just above, in the place where this note is marked in the text, I emphasize these cumbersome "quasis" that I take on so often. On *deconstruction and radicality*, and for the sake of brevity, within such limits, I will simply refer you to, among my more recent work, *Specters of Marx*.

[16] Especially in *The Tain of the Mirror, Derrida and the Philosophy of Reflection* (Cambridge: Harvard University Press, 1986).

[17] *Of Grammatology*, trans. Gayatri Spivak (Baltimore: Johns Hopkins University Press, 1974).

[18] Beyond the luminous readings with which, for several years – cf. in particular his book *La passion de l'origine* (Galilée, 1995), and his articles in *Le passage des frontières* and *Passions de la littérature*, (Galilée 1994 and 1996) – Giovannangeli has called me back to a Sartrian legacy which I can, thanks to him, reinterpret, I would have liked to pursue here the discussion of the possible-impossible as the law of desire or of love (in Heidegger and in relation to another thought of the *Ereignis* – whether or not one translates this word as "event"). I would do it, if the space and the time were given to us, by considering what Giovannangeli develops around the "possibility of an unconscious affect."

[19] To say or to write is at once to assume the legacy of natural language and of ordinary language *while formalizing them*, by folding them to fit this formalizing abstraction of which they originally carry the power: the use of a word or phrase, however simple and ordinary they might be, the putting into play of their power, is already, through the identification of iterable words, a formalizing idealization; there is thus no *purely* ordinary language any more than there is any *purely* philosophical language, any formal language, or, in any sense of the word, an extraordinary language. In this sense, if it is true, as Austin says, that there isn't any "last word," it is difficult to say, as he does, that ordinary language is the "*first* word," a word simply and indivisibly "first."

[20] *Passions* (Galilée, 1993) 26 n.5 p. 81. I also examined the Foucauldian notion of "problematization" in "Etre juste avec Freud", in *Résistances – de la Psychanalyse* (Galilée 1996) 142-143.

[21] Cf. in particular *Of Spirit*, notably the discussion of the promise, the yes prior to any opposition of yes and no, and especially that which comes "before any question" (p.147sq); and *Politics of Friendship*, *passim*.

[22] On the repetition of this "yes, yes", see my *Ulysse Gramophone, Deux mots pour Joyce* (Galilée, 1987) 132 sq and *passim*, as well as "Nombre de oui" in *Psyché*.

[23] "Violence and Metaphysics" in Alan Bass, trans., *Writing and Difference* (Chicago: University of Chicago Press, 1978) 79.

[24] *Writing and Difference*, 79-80.

[25] *Given Time: I. Counterfeit Money*, trans. Peggy Kamuf (Chicago: University of Chicago Press, 1992) 29.

[26] "Ousia and Grammè: Note on a Note from *Being and Time*" in *Margins of Philosophy*, trans. Alan Bass (Chicago: University of Chicago Press, 1982) 29.

[27] "Ousia and Grammè", 55.

[28] "Inventions of the other", 60.

[29] *The Post Card*, trans. Alan Bass (Chicago: University of Chicago Press, 1987).

[30] *The Post Card*, 489.

[31] *The Post Card*, 30.

[32] *The Post Card*.

[33] English in the original.

[34] On this impossible possibility, this im-possibility as pervertibility, as the permanent possibility of the perverse transformation of the promise into a threat, see "Avances," Preface to S. Margel, *Le tombeau du Dieu artisan* (Paris: Minuit, 1995).

[35] Some time ago, in the space of Husserlian phenomenology, I analyzed in an analogous fashion an apparently negative possibility of form, an im-possibility, the impossibility of full and immediate intuition, the "essential possibility of non-intuition", the

"possibility of the crisis" as a "crisis of the logos". But this possibility of the impossibility, I said at the time, isn't simply negative; the trap also becomes a chance: "for Husserl, this possibility [of the crisis] remains connected, to the very moment of truth and the production of ideal objectivity; it has in fact an essential need for writing" (*Of Grammatology*, 40; and especially *Introduction à l'origine de la géométrie de Husserl* (Paris: PUF, 1962).

[36] English in the original.

[37] Both English in the original.

[38] "The ultimate aporia is the impossibility of the aporia *as such*", *Apories* (Paris: Galilée 1993) 137. Another way of emphasizing that there is no question without a problem, but no problem that doesn't hide or protect itself behind the possibility of an answer.

[39] English in the original.

[40] "Différance", 1967, in *Margins of Philosophy*, tr. Alan Bass (University of Chicago Press 1982).

[41] One can consult the numerous and admirable works of Plotnitsky, especially *In the Shadow of Hegel: Complementarity, History and the Unconscious* (Gainesville: Florida University Press, 1993), *Complementarity: Anti-epistemology after Bohr and Derrida* (Durham, NC: Duke University Press, 1994), as well as his masterful interventions, more recently, concerning the so-called "Sokal Affair". Since Christopher Norris has just published (in the perspective of the article that can be read here) an important work in which he devotes a chapter to quantum mechanics, the interested reader can look there for a friendly, and fundamentally concordant, discussion of certain aspects of Plotnitsky's interpretation. Norris regrets that this interpretation is sometimes "more postmodernist than deconstructive", but nonetheless praises his work (*Against Relativism, Philosophy of Science, Deconstruction and Critical Theory*, [Blackwell, 1997] 113). Although I don't share Norris's reservations, the space of this problematic and of this discussion seems to me to be of a major necessity today. As for me, I always learn a great deal at these various crossroads: of deconstruction and the sciences, undoubtedly, but also of two approaches – certainly very different, those of Norris and Plotnitsky – I would like to salute here. Nobody is doing more and better today than these two philosophers to dissipate the tenacious prejudices ("deconstruction" is foreign or hostile to "science," or "reason", that deconstruction, as I mentioned earlier, is "empiricist", "skeptical," or "relativist", "a game" or "nihilist", "antihumanist", and so on). No one demonstrates better than they the necessity and the fecundity of the co-implications between "deconstructive" and "scientific" problematics, which are too often separated. In discussions but also in institutions.

[42] *Of Grammatology*, 93.

[43] I emphasize the words that make reference here to these three instances, thought, philosophy and science: "Derrida's work reflects or mediates aspects of contemporary science. It deals of course with only one dimension of his work, but it does show a *thinker* open to the implications of science." And Johnson goes on to specify this, which I want to emphasize because it raises the prejudice according to which "science doesn't think" (Heidegger): "open to the implications of science, of what science gives us to think." How does science "give" to think? Beyond "such limits", I would have liked to develop this analysis in terms of this "give" and this "gift" (*donation*).

[44] Cf. "Foi et savoir. Les deux sources de la 'religion' aux limites de la simple raison" In *La Religion*, J. Derrida and G. Vattimo, eds (Seuil, 1996).

Index

alphabet 71
alterity 76
analogy 14–28, 99, 110–11
answers 1, 3–4, 97–8, 104
anti-relativism 39
apodicticity 2–3
apprehension 35
Aristotle 2, 36, 41–61
autre temps 29–30, 31

Bachelard, G. 44, 52
Bataille, G. 74–5
Bateson, 86
being 32, 51
belief 47, 51
Benjamin, 91
Benveniste, E. 41–50
Bhaskar, R. 44, 60–61
biology 85, 88

Canguilhem, G. 45, 52
categories 41–2, 43, 50, 54
chance 68
chorology 35
closure 77–9
code 89–90
concepts 31, 39, 45–6, 48–9, 52–3, 68, 103
consciousness 6, 10, 41
contradiction 2
cosmology 22
counterpoint 69
cwvra 29–37
cybernetics 85

Davidson, D. 40, 58

deconstruction 1, 3, 14, 55, 78
delay 6, 8, 10, 104
Deleuze, G. 68, 69
Descartes, R. 3
destination 107
dialectics 9, 16, 75
différance 2, 10, 14, 66–79, 112
dignity 33
discourse 47
dissemination 23, 77, 89
distance 73
double analogy 54
dreaming 29, 34–7

economy 74–6, 113
empirical 41–4
(en)closure 77–8
error 108
etymology 55
events 96, 113
excess 32–3, 34
excuses 98

facilitation 86
facticity 9
failure 109
figurative 4
forgiveness 101–2
foundationalism, rejection of 1
Freud, S. 6–7, 85–8

Gasch,, R. 103
genealogy 24
Genet, J. 66
genetics 88–90
gift 106

Index

Glaucon 33, 35
good 33, 34
Gorgias 17–22
Goux, J.J. 85
grammatology 76

Habermas, J. 4
Hegel, G.W.F. 66–79
Heidegger, M. 66
Husserl, E. 7–8

imagination 31
immortality 24
impossible 101–2, 106–9
impression 7
information 86
intentionality 9
invention 107
irony 19–20
iterability 40

khora 31, 99, 111
knowledge 44, 46
kosmos 18, 20–21
Koyre, A. 72

language 4, 40, 41–50, 56, 97, 100
language-game 47
last word 96
life 88
literality 4
locus 32, 35
logical empiricism 42, 43
logocentrism 74, 113
logos 2, 16, 19–23, 24, 99

meaning 40
meaning-holism 42
melody 7
memory 86
memory trace 86
metaphor 113

metaphors 33–4, 39, 44, 46, 48–9, 52–60, 68, 88–90
metaphysics 39, 51, 77–8
mimesis 59–60
mind 47
modal logic 53
models 52
Mystic Writing Pad 87

names 4, 56–7, 72
necessity 2–3, 110
Nietzsche, F. 45
nouns 59

ontology 8, 9
ontotheology 74
ordinary language 97

paradigm 47
perception 35
perhaps 96–7
pharmakon 14–20, 23, 24, 99
phenomenology 8
philosophy 39
place 35
Plato 2, 114–28, 60
play 68
pleasure 6
poetry 60
point 68–9
position 68
possible 100–1, 109
    see also impossible
predicates 41–2, 43
presence 74
priority 59
privilege philosophy 39
problematization 3, 104–5
proportionality 15
propositionality 1–2, 104
Protagoras 21–2
protention 9

proximity 73
quantum mechanics 50, 114
quasi-propositions 102–3
questions 1, 3–5, 16, 99, 105

realism 46
reality 39
rectification 45–6, 52
reminiscence 6–7
response 97–8, 100
retention 9
rhetoric 4, 22
Rorty, R. 39
Russell, B. 47

Sartre, J.P. 8–9
Schiffer, S. 40
science 44, 52, 84–94, 114
scientific discourse 45–6
scientific truth 47
seed metaphor 88–9
semantics 40, 53
sentences 4
signifier 70
Socrates 2, 16–21, 33–5
soul 22
sovereignty 75
space 17
speech 17–18, 70, 76, 97

speech-acts 40
structuralism 47, 56, 84
supplement 14
supplementarity 73
survival 91

technology 87
temporality 6–7, 9
text 47
thought 29, 41, 45, 50, 114
Timaeus 15, 29–30, 36
time 30
tovpoi 35–6
traces 3, 6, 14
transaction 110
transcendental 9, 50, 103
transcendental argument 42
translation 72–3, 91
truth 47, 59
truth-value 53

unconscious 6, 43–4

voice 17

Wilden, 87
Wittgenstein, L. 5
writing 9, 14, 17, 22–3, 39, 70–71, 76–7, 84, 87–8

For Product Safety Concerns and Information please contact our EU
representative GPSR@taylorandfrancis.com
Taylor & Francis Verlag GmbH, Kaufingerstraße 24, 80331 München, Germany